The World of Cooking

The World of Cooking

based on the television series created
by Hal and Marilyn Weiner

Introduction and commentary by
Derek Cooper

British Broadcasting Corporation

Published to accompany the television series,
The World of Cooking, first broadcast on
BBC1 in January 1984

Illustrated by Christopher Brown

Recipes edited by Moya Maynard

© The Hal and Marilyn Weiner Production Company 1983
First published 1983
Reprinted 1983

Published by the
British Broadcasting Corporation
35 Marylebone High Street
London W1M 4AA

Photoset in 11pt Plantin Light and Bold by Ace Filmsetting
Printed in England by Belmont Press and Pitman Press
ISBN 0 563 21009 5

Contents

Italy
Bolognese Sauce 54
Besciamella Sauce *Basic white sauce* 55
Tagliolini Verdi Gratinati 56
Scampi alla Carlina 57
Risi e Bisi *Venetian risotto* 58
Fegato alla Veneziana con Polenta
Venetian liver with corn bread 59
Crespelli *Pancakes* 61

Mexico
Guacamole *Avocado dip* 64
Sopa de Medula *Beef marrow soup* 65
Pollo en Manchamenteles *Chicken stewed with fruit* 66
Sopes de Chorizo con Papas
Tortillas with sausage and potatoes 67
Salsa Verde *Green tomato sauce* 68
Filete de Robalo Veracruzana
Sea bass Vera-Cruz style 69
Dulce de Coco Piña *Sweet coconut with pineapple* 70

Hong Kong
Crabmeat and Vegetables 73
Duck with Water Chestnuts 74
Fried Sea Bass 76
West Lake Beef Soup 77
Pineapple Fried Rice 78

India
Mutton Kofta Curry *Meatballs* 80
Puri *Fried bread puffs* 81
Aloo Gobi *Spiced potato and cauliflower* 83
Sarsoon Sag *Mustard greens* 84
Mughlai Chicken 85
Jalebis *Deep-fried pretzel-shaped sweets* 87

Japan
Wakadori Kuwayaki *Chicken in soy sauce* 89
Oshi Zushi *Pressed rice and mackerel* 90
Yakimono *Grilled steak* 91
Tempura *Batter-fried food* 92
Kamo Nabe *Cook-it-yourself duck* 94

Introduction

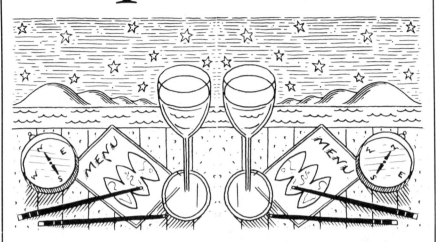

In Singapore recently I was interested to see Kentucky Fried Chicken franchises and McDonald hamburger take-aways. 'A pity the world is getting so small,' said a friend, 'before long our own kind of food will just disappear.'

I don't agree. Indeed the recipes in this book reveal just how strong and historic are the influences of cross-fertilisation when it comes to the world of cooking. As soon as the first traveller got on his horse or sailed over the horizon the changes began. Marco Polo is reputed to have brought the secret of spaghetti back from his Far Eastern journeys. Did he? Nobody really knows, but the resemblances between the *pasta* of Italy, the *soba* and *udon* of Japan and the noodles of China are remarkable.

The Moghuls altered the cooking of India, and when the Spaniards discovered the Americas there was an almost instant revolution in Europe. It was the Aztec and Mayan civilisations which gave us such things as the tomato, the turkey and the avocado. When Montezuma presented the Spanish conquistadors with the cocoa bean they brought it back, added vanilla and sugar, and chocolate was born. *Polenta* which has been a part of the Italian diet for four hundred years was first brought to Venice in the form of maize from the New World. *Tempura*, the very Japanese technique of frying fish and vegetables in batter, didn't exist until Spanish and Portuguese missionaries took the secret to the East in the sixteenth century.

Chef Carlos Santis preparing a speciality of Sitges may well ponder on its origins. Is it really Catalonian or are its roots to be found thousands of miles from Spain? 'The only other cuisine I know,' says Carlos, 'that combines lobster and chicken is the Chinese. I wonder if our Catalonian explorers brought the recipe back with them . . . or maybe it was the other way around.' Whatever the origin, the final touch – half an ounce of chocolate – is unmistakably Aztec.

So the world of cooking is full of serendipity; the *nasi goreng* you eat in Malacca bears a strong resemblance to the *paella* of Valencia; the *bouillabaisse* of Marseilles is mirrored in fish stews from Japan to Brazil. An even more important influence is the single-mindedness of the world's great chefs, whether they are preparing vegetarian food in north India or *nouvelle cuisine* in France.

All of them are using the best and freshest raw materials; all of them are striving for simplicity, and all of them regard cooking as an art not a science. It is in Japan that the skills of the cook are made most manifest as an art form. Nabuo Iida, our Tokyo chef, talks of *moritsuke* – the arrangement of food to give as much aesthetic pleasure as the texture and taste. 'For us,' he says, 'food must do more than simply ease hunger. Good chefs automatically think of presentation – colour, design, depth.' Even when it comes to the paring of a carrot, the act is performed so that the final shape complements the function of the vegetable and its impact on the tastebuds.

Carrying things a bit too far? If it is, then it is a fancy shared by all the chefs in this book. As our Finnish cook Reijo Rajala says, 'If a dish is pleasing to the eye, it should be pleasing to the palate.' And Hans Clemens in Amsterdam compares himself with his fellow artists, Rembrandt and Van Gogh.

Although the chefs speak many different languages, their attitude to food is identical. 'Chinese cooking,' says Hong Kong chef Leung Ting-Kee, 'is very much like a performing art.

Things happen quickly and one must be ready to do what has to be done.' Artist and actor in a continually changing drama – that's how great chefs see themselves. 'I love to cook at people's tables,' says Japanese master chef Nabuo Iida. 'I suppose all chefs like to perform before a live audience.'

What excites them is their ability to improvise and create, and they all have the same message – don't cook by numbers. A recipe is no more than a map; it only indicates where you should go. Your own personality makes the journey successful.

Carlos Santis, the chef who has prepared the Spanish dishes, talking about *sopa de pescado* claimed that if you asked a hundred chefs what really goes into a fish stock you would get a hundred different answers: 'But if you ask one hundred Catalonians you will get three hundred answers – one recipe for himself, one for his grandmother and one for his wife.'

Similarly, when our French chef André Revest is at work in his kitchen in St Pierre de Chartreuse, he is working more with his eyes and his palate than with a pair of scales. How much salt for the *truite à la pâte d'amandes*? 'A large pinch. Good cooks don't measure things exactly. It is an intuition, just as an artist or a musician must *feel* when things are right.'

Here then are the ingredients and the directions; all you add is the artistry. Eat well.

Derek Cooper

Note

Some of the recipes in this book may differ slightly from those in the television series. They have been adapted to include ingredients available in the United Kingdom.

When cooking, do not mix the metric and imperial measures, but stick to one system or the other.

Spain

The oldest printed cookery book in Spain is written in Catalan. Catalonia is an autonomous region which shares the traditions of *la buena mesa* with the rest of the country, but likes to think that its food is the best. Olive oil, garlic, peppers, almonds, saffron and parsley form the basis of many dishes, but there is an old tradition of combining meat with fruit and seafood with poultry, and Catalonia has its own white sausage, *butifarra*, spiced with nutmeg, cinnamon, cloves and thyme.

It is a very individual style of cooking and Carlos Santis, chef of the Calipolis restaurant in Sitges, is aware both of its differences from and similarities to that of the rest of Spain. 'Though I like to think of my cooking as Catalonian, I must say that here in Spain there are many similarities in the kitchens of different regions. But when I am working in my kitchen, I am a Catalan first and a Spaniard second. All Spanish cooking is really what we call *del pueblo*, food of the people. We don't have the tradition of a *grande cuisine* like our neighbours to the north. But of even more importance, eating for us is a social occasion, a joyous festivity, a chance for friends and family to relax.'

●

Catalonian Bread

A typical Catalonian meal begins with a selection of hors d'oeuvres called *entremeses*. Because Carlos Santis has chosen a fairly hearty meal, his first course is a simple and cheap bread dish: 'A great favourite in Sitges, it's easy to make, fool-proof really. The only danger is that one can eat too much – so just one slice per person!'

4 large slices of light sour dough or rye bread	salt
	a little olive oil
2 large cloves garlic	
2 medium sized tomatoes, skinned	*Serves 4*

1 Lightly toast the bread on both sides.

2 Peel the garlic, cut in half and rub each slice of bread well with the cut side of garlic.

3 Cut each tomato in half and mash each half onto a piece of toast.

4 Sprinkle with a little salt and olive oil.

Note Depending on the size of the slices of bread, more tomato may be used and the slices halved. If light rye bread is unobtainable, any firm bread will do.

Sopa de Pescado
Fish soup

The classic Catalan dish is *sopa de pescado*. 'Catalonia was once united with France,' says Carlos. 'That was many centuries ago. It may explain why we have been accused of borrowing from the French. I choose to believe it is the other way around. This soup is similar to the French *bouillabaisse*. It may be called Catalan *bullabesa*. But here in Catalan we are very choosy about what we put in our soup. I have heard that in Marseilles they are not so particular!'

2 tablespoons olive oil	8 oz (225 g) fresh squid (backbone removed), sliced
4 oz (125 g) onion, chopped	
3 cloves garlic, crushed	12 oz (375 g) cooked crayfish
1 oz (25 g) finely chopped parsley	2 fl oz (50 ml) brandy (optional)
12 small fresh clams, steamed until just opened	15 fl oz (425 ml) fish stock
	2½ tablespoons anise
8 oz (225 g) fresh or frozen scallops	salt
	2 oz (50 g) cooked rice (optional)
8 oz (225 g) cooked shrimps or peeled prawns	*Serves 6*

1 In a large heavy pan, heat the oil, add the chopped onion, garlic and parsley, cook gently to soften without colouring, then draw pan off the heat.

2 Add the clams to the pan with the scallops (halved if large) and the sliced squid. Stir. Add the cooked shrimps or prawns, and crayfish to the pan. Cook over a high heat for 2 minutes, pour in the brandy, if using, and flame.

3 Stir in the fish stock, bring to the boil and season to taste with salt and anise. Simmer for 5 minutes.

4 Stir in cooked rice, if liked.

Note Prepare the stock in advance using local fish, bones or skins, cover with water, add a peeled sliced carrot, onion and garlic with parsley, almonds and saffron if liked.

If clams are unavailable, use fresh mussels.

●

Escalibada
Mixed grilled vegetables

Escalibada is a popular dish that can be served for *tapas* – the snacks you take with an aperitif – or as a vegetable course in the middle of a meal. Aubergine, sweet red peppers, onions and tomatoes are grilled over charcoal, peeled, salted and served warm or cold. 'This rustic style of cooking dates back to the days when charcoal fires were an inexpensive source of heat. Catalonians, known for their thriftiness, used them for cooking as well. But the real key to this dish – and in fact all great cooking – is to use what is in season and what is fresh,' explains Carlos Santis.

8 oz (225 g) aubergine (preferably a long thin one)	2 large tomatoes
	salt and olive oil to taste
8 oz (225 g) red pepper	
8 oz (225 g) onion, optional	*Serves 4–6*

1 *Either* grill the vegetables whole over a charcoal barbecue for about 30 minutes until tender so that the skins will easily peel off; *or* cut the aubergine, onion and pepper in half lengthwise and grill, skin side up, under a high heat for about 15 minutes until the skin scorches and blisters easily and peels. Dip the tomatoes in boiling water for a few seconds.

2 Peel the vegetables, slice thinly (discarding seeds from pepper) then arrange in rows on a serving plate.

3 Sprinkle vegetables with olive oil and salt to taste. Serve chilled.

●

Chicken and Lobster Subur Style

This dish combines fresh whole lobster, chicken and chocolate. The base is Romesco sauce, similar to the creole Remoulade sauce popular in New Orleans. Carlos Santis explains: 'The spiciness of this sauce varies from hot to mild just as peppers do, and everyone has his own opinion about which is best. In fact I've heard it said that finding a Romesco sauce to please everyone is as difficult as finding three good matadors in one afternoon's bullfight. Subur was the ancient Roman name of Sitges. But the unusual ingredient, chocolate, was introduced to Spain much later by our explorers in the New World. In general, cooking meat with chocolate is a Spanish speciality, something we learned from the Aztecs who were the first to cook sauces with the cocoa bean.'

Romesco sauce	1–1½ lb (450–675 g) live lobster
8 fl oz (225 ml) olive or cooking oil	salt and pepper
	flour for dredging
1 fresh chilli, finely chopped	2 tablespoons cooking oil
4 oz (125 g) red pepper, coarsely chopped	2¼ lb (1 kg) fresh chicken cut into 8 small joints
5 cloves garlic, crushed	½ oz (15 g) drinking chocolate
2 oz (50 g) onion, finely chopped	
12 blanched almonds, browned under grill	
12 oz (375 g) fresh tomatoes, skinned	
2 fl oz (50 ml) red wine vinegar	*Serves 4–6*

1 Place 2 tablespoons of the measured oil in a heavy saucepan and cook the chilli, peppers, garlic, onion and almonds over a very low heat for about 20 minutes or until soft and pulpy, stirring occasionally.

2 Add the tomatoes and vinegar to the pan and continue to cook for a further 15 minutes.

3 Pour this mixture into a strainer over a bowl, press through as much liquid as possible. Add 4 tablespoons of the oil and push this through also. Keep this strained Romesco sauce on one side.

4 Place the live lobster on a board with the spine uppermost. Quickly and firmly insert a sharp heavy knife just below the centre of the head and continue to cut the lobster in half lengthwise.

5 Discard head end, removing intestines and tract which is the dark line running the length of the body.

6 Cut claws off by placing knife over a joint and hitting sharply with a hammer. Lightly crack claws.

7 Sprinkle the pieces of lobster and chicken with salt, and dredge lightly with flour.

8 Heat the remaining oil in a heavy frying pan, put in the lobster and fry, turning frequently for 5 minutes until the white flesh is opaque and lightly browned. Remove into a shallow casserole dish.

9 Add the chicken pieces to the pan, cook over a fairly high heat turning frequently for 15–20 minutes or until cooked, add to the lobster.

10 Cool the pan slightly and sprinkle in the chocolate, blending this into the pan juices.

11 Stir in 8 fl oz (225 ml) of the reserved sauce, cook gently until heated through, add salt and pepper.

12 Preheat oven to 425°F (220°C), gas mark 7, centre shelf.

13 Pour sauce over the meats to coat, and bake for about 15 minutes until piping hot. Serve with boiled rice.

Note If fresh lobster is difficult to obtain use 4 large prawn tails.

●

Peaches in Wine

Chef Santis likes to combine local sweet wines with fruit to make this simple and uncomplicated dessert.

4 large ripe peaches	2 rounded teaspoons caster sugar
8 fl oz (225 ml) sweet wine	*Serves 3–4*

1 Cut the peaches in half with a stainless steel knife. Twist the halves apart.

2 Peel peaches, remove stones, then cut pieces in half again.

3 Place peach quarters in a bowl, pour over the wine and stir in the sugar.

4 Chill peaches for 30 minutes before serving.

Brazil

Soon after the Portuguese moved into Brazil they began importing slaves from West Africa to work on the sugar plantations. The slaves, bringing with them their own food preferences and cooking techniques, soon found that tropical Brazil was similar enough in climate to Africa to produce the plants of their homeland – yams, okra, bananas, peanuts, palm trees for palm oil (or *dende*) and coconuts.

Africans did most of the cooking in Brazil until 1888 when slavery was abolished, producing a unique Afro-Portuguese mutation. In this way they shaped the cuisine of Bahia, the Brazilian state from which this menu comes. Coupled to this was the influence of the native Indians whose greatest contribution was the use of manioc meal from the cassava plant. Roberto Campos cooks Bahian food with great flair, and he has prepared a fairly typical feast. 'Bahian cooking,' he says, 'is remarkable for its extraordinary colour and taste. How we Brazilians love to eat!'

Casquinha de Siri
Baked stuffed crab

Brazil's most popular first course is *casquinha de siri*, baked stuffed crab, a dish with its origins in West Africa. 'It's a wonderful beginning, lovely to look at, delicious, full of taste,' says Roberto Campos.

2 oz (50 g) onion, chopped	4 fl oz (125 ml) coconut milk
2 cloves garlic, finely chopped	1–2 teaspoons paprika
2 tablespoons cooking oil	fresh white breadcrumbs
1 lb (450 g) prepared white crabmeat	Tabasco sauce
	salt
1 tomato, peeled and chopped	2 oz (50 g) grated cheese
2 tablespoons chopped chives	
2 tablespoons chopped parsley	*Serves 4–6*

1 Gently fry the onion and garlic in the oil, stirring until lightly browned.

2 Stir in the crabmeat, tomato, chopped chives and parsley. Stir well together.

3 Mix in the coconut milk, paprika and breadcrumbs then season with Tabasco sauce and salt to taste. Stir over a low heat for about 5 minutes.

4 Divide the mixture between 4–6 scallop shells, scatter with the cheese, then grill for 3–5 minutes under a high heat.

5 Serve the shells piping hot garnished with lemon wedges.

Note Coconut milk is available in Oriental shops or in some health food stores. Otherwise use creamed coconut diluted with water. Ramekin dishes can be used instead of scallop shells.

Xinxim de Galinha
Chicken with peanuts

Xinxim de galinha is a special Bahian dish that combines flavours in an unusual way. Chicken, peanuts and coconut milk may not, at first, sound attractive, but try it.

3–3½ lb (1½ kg) fresh chicken	2 oz (50 g) peanuts, minced
juice of half a lemon	4 tablespoons parsley, freshly
salt	chopped
4 tablespoons groundnut oil	1 large tomato, finely chopped
8 oz (225 g) onion, chopped	4 fl oz (100 ml) coconut milk
4 spring onions, chopped	Tabasco sauce to taste
4 cloves garlic, finely chopped	pepper
4 oz (125 g) green pepper, chopped	*Serves 6*

1 Cut the chicken into 6 joints, arrange on a plate and sprinkle with the lemon juice and some salt. Leave aside for a while for the chicken to absorb the lemon flavour.

2 Using a large cast iron casserole, heat the oil and fry the chicken for about 10 minutes to brown on all sides.

3 Add the onion, spring onion and garlic, fry for a few minutes, then add the green pepper and peanuts. Cover and cook gently until the onion is soft. (It may be necessary to remove the chicken while the vegetables are softening.)

4 Add parsley and tomato to the casserole, the coconut milk and tabasco.

5 Cover casserole, reduce heat and cook slowly until chicken is tender.

6 Lift chicken into hot serving dish. Season sauce to taste, pour over chicken and sprinkle with extra chopped parsley, if liked. Serve immediately.

Moqueca de Camarão
Prawn stew

Brazil has a coastline 3500 miles long, and the annual fishing catch exceeds two million tons. In the north-east, particularly, shellfish abound and Brazilian 'shrimps' (large prawns) and lobsters are exported all over the world. So much is netted that much of it is dried and ground up for use in all sorts of recipes.

The indigenous Indians lived on fish. The Portuguese with their long coastline and cod-fishing traditions were equally fond of it, and the West Africans adapted it to their own style of cooking. This next dish, *moqueca de camarão*, gets its name from an ancient Indian dish called *pokekas*. The Indians used to roast their highly-spiced, peppery food in banana leaves over charcoal fires. The African slaves added *dende* oil, hot peppers and coconut milk, and over the years these combinations of ingredients came to be cooked in pots the Portuguese way.

Today this stew is one of the most famous dishes in the Bahian repertoire.

3 tablespoons oil	1 large tomato, chopped
4 oz (125 g) green pepper, deseeded and chopped	2 tablespoons fresh parsley, finely chopped
1 clove garlic, crushed	4 fl oz (125 ml) coconut milk
4 oz (125 g) onion, chopped	Tabasco to taste
8–12 oz (225–375 g) peeled prawns (if frozen, thaw and drain)	salt
	Serves 4

1 Heat the oil in a shallow pan. Add the chopped green pepper, garlic and onion. Fry gently until soft.

2 Stir in the prawns, tomato, parsley, coconut milk, Tabasco and salt. Cover pan and cook gently for 5 minutes to heat the prawns through.

3 Serve with plain boiled rice.

Doce de Banana
Banana sweet

All over Brazil innumerable banana groves provide an instant and nutritious meal, and the banana is the basic fruit for many desserts. Nothing could be simpler than *doce de banana*.

8 oz (225 g) demerara sugar	6 cloves
¾ pint (375 ml) warm water	5 bananas, peeled and cut crosswise
2 cinnamon sticks	*Serves 4*

1 Place the sugar and water in a saucepan. Stir to dissolve.

2 Add remaining ingredients, cover and cook *very* gently for about 2 hours.

3 Spoon bananas into a dish, pour over the cooking liquid and leave to stand for 10 minutes before serving.

Note If liquid evaporates, add a little more water to thin it down.

Finland

Finland, the most northerly country in this book, has nine months of winter and only three months in which to enjoy the fruits of the earth. Maybe that's why they welcome summer so enthusiastically, as a time to decamp to the countryside, drink in the warm sun and revel in home-grown strawberries, wild morel mushrooms and Arctic cloudberries. Since the sun never really sets, the twenty-two hours of sun that fruit and vegetables receive every day makes them ripen quickly, and gives them an extra sweetness.

The most typical feature of a Finnish meal is the *smörgåsbord*, laid with fish, meat, eggs, salads and cheeses – an elaborate assortment meant as an appetiser, but which can be sufficient for an entire meal. The most important fish in Finland is the herring, although salmon takes pride of place on special occasions.

Gravlax
Salmon in dill

Reijo Rajala, head-chef of the famous seaside hotel
Kalastajatorppa, or 'fisherman's cottage', usually starts a
special meal with Finland's favourite appetiser, *gravlax* –
salmon sprinkled with sea salt and sugar, and flavoured with
sprigs of fresh dill. Dill is the dominant seasoning in
Scandinavian cooking – as popular with Finns as parsley or
mint is here. It is found in pickles, soups, stews and sauces.

1 young salmon weighing 2–2½ lb (1 kg)	1 teaspoon white peppercorns, freshly ground
4 teaspoons coarse sea salt	a good bunch of fresh dill
2 teaspoons granulated sugar	*Serves about 10–12 portions*

1 Ask the fishmonger to gut and fillet the fish for you. Or,
using a sharp boning knife, carefully cut each side of the
backbone to give 2 fillets, remove any bony sections along the
sides of the fillet.

2 Lay the fillets flesh side uppermost and sprinkle each
liberally with the salt and pat it in.

3 Sprinkle the sugar and peppers evenly over the fillets.

4 Wash the dill and spread the sprigs all over the fish.

5 Place the fillets together tail end to head end, flesh sides
together, and wrap tightly in greaseproof paper.

6 Store in a cool place, about 55°F (18°C), for at least 1 or 2
days, with a heavy platter on top to press in the herbs.

7 Unwrap the fish, pour off any liquid that may have formed.

8 Pat the fish dry with kitchen paper and scrape off any excess
salt and the dill.

9 To serve, cut the flesh in paper-thin slices commencing near
the tail end and cutting towards the tail, so that the flesh will
not fall apart.

10 Slice and roll up 2 or 3 slices per person, as a starter, or
more slices per person if serving as part of a smörgåsbord or
light main course.

Korvasienimuhennos
Creamed mushrooms

The vegetables that traditionally accompany *gravlax* are new potatoes and creamed mushrooms. Finns like to use morels, which are a pungent wild variety of mushroom, but most mushrooms will be fine in this recipe. 'Take care not to overcook your mushrooms,' says Reijo, 'you don't want them to shrink, lose their texture or change their colour.'

3 oz (75 g) butter	4 level tablespoons plain flour
2 medium sized onions, finely chopped	½ pint (275 ml) double cream
	salt and pepper
1½ lb (675 g) open mushrooms, washed	*Serves 4–6*

1 Melt the butter in a large saucepan, add the onions, cook until soft without browning for about 5 minutes.

2 Cut the mushrooms in quarters, if large, and add to the onion. Stir round and cook for about 3 minutes over a moderately high flame, so that they are coated in the butter.

3 Blend the flour gradually into the cream and add to the mushrooms.

4 Stir gently to mix. Bring slowly to the boil while stirring. Simmer for 5 minutes.

5 Add salt and pepper to taste.

Uudet Perunet
New potatoes

This dish can only be done with new potatoes – it is not necessary to remove the skins and if dill is not available, parsley is a good substitute.

2 lb (1 kg) small new potatoes	fresh dill
1 teaspoon sea salt	*Serves 4*

1 Scrub the potatoes (or scrape if preferred).

2 Bring a saucepan of water to the boil with the salt, add the potatoes and the stalks from the dill

3 Partially cover and simmer for 15–20 minutes until just tender.

4 Drain well and sprinkle with roughly chopped dill and butter if liked.

Lohikeitto
Salmon soup

Soups play an important role in Finnish cooking; some of them are eaten as a first course, others are so robust they constitute an entire meal. 'When men get together in Finland,' says Reijo Rajala, 'and the talk turns to food, you can be sure that soup will come up early in the conversation. It seems that many of our dishes were created with men in mind. It's said in northern Finland that a man needs to eat six bowls of soup every day – three for the flavour and three more to fill up!'

A popular soup is *lohikeitto* made with salmon, but pike, perch or white fish make perfectly good alternatives. 'Just remember that fresh fish means a richer taste and a better soup. The flavour of the fish stock varies with its ingredients, so no two stocks are ever exactly alike. Each batch gets its flavour from the type of fish used.'

1 lb (450 g) salmon, pike, perch or carp to give 12 oz (375 g) after trimming	12 oz (375 g) potatoes, sliced
	salt and pepper
	$4 \times \frac{1}{2}$ inch (1 cm) thick slices black ryebread
2 oz (50 g) butter	
12 oz (375 g) onions, chopped	5 fl oz (150 ml) carton single cream
3 bayleaves	
6 allspice berries	2 tablespoons chopped parsley
fish stock (made from the fish trimmings)	
	Serves 4–6

1 Remove skin and bone from fish and place in saucepan, cover with cold water and cook gently to make fish stock $1\frac{3}{4}$ pints (1 litre).

2 Cut fish into cubes.

3 Melt the butter in a fairly large saucepan, add the onions, cook gently until soft without browning.

4 Add bayleaves, allspice and fish stock.

5 Stir in potatoes, add a little salt and the cubed fish, cover and bring to a gentle simmer. Cook for 10 minutes.

6 Arrange the bread in a single layer in the soup. Leave in long enough for the soup to absorb some of the smoky flavour of the bread.

7 Remove the bread slices with a slotted spoon and discard.

8 Stir in the cream, parsley and seasonings to taste. Heat through for a few seconds and serve with fresh black ryebread.

Karjalanpiirakat
Karelian pastries

Chef Rajala specialises in Karelian pastries, and he's especially fond of rice pastries. It is customary to serve Karelian pastries hot from the oven with egg butter.

Dough	Filling
4 fl oz (100 ml) cold water	6 fl oz (175 ml) water
1 teaspoon salt	5 oz (150 g) pudding rice
6 oz (175 g) rye flour	4 tablespoons milk
1½ oz (40 g) plain white flour	salt to taste
	Makes 6

1 To make the dough, combine all the ingredients and mix to a pliable dough. Cover and chill for 30 minutes.

2 Make the filling: place all the ingredients in a non-stick pan, cook very gently until tender for about ¾ hour, stirring occasionally. Allow to cool.

3 Divide the pastry into six, and roll each piece into an oval or boat shape.

4 Divide the cooled rice into six and arrange along the centre of each piece of pastry.

5 Pinch the ends together and crimp along the top so that some of the rice shows.

6 Place on floured baking sheet and cook in a hot oven 450°F (230°C), gas mark 8 for 10–15 minutes.

7 Serve hot in a folded napkin with egg butter as an hors d'oeuvre or an accompaniment to meat.

Egg Butter

2 or 3 hard boiled eggs, sieved	salt and pepper
8 oz (225 g) softened butter	

Stir these together with a little salt and pepper.

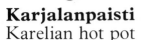

Karjalanpaisti
Karelian hot pot

In the long cold winter nights Finns turn to soups, hearty stews and roasts. In Reijo Rajala's view nothing compares with Karelian Hot Pot: 'On Independence Day each year, I go home and make this stew for my family, and we eat the meal in silence. It's a Finnish tradition to celebrate our independence quietly. Even our parades are quiet.'

In the past, Karelian cooks would put casseroles in the oven early in the evening while the stove was still warm from baking the daily bread. In the morning the slowly cooked meat was tender enough to part with a fork. 'It isn't necessary to season this dish with a heavy hand,' Reijo warns, 'because slow cooking allows the flavours of the three meats to blend.'

1 lb (450 g) lean pork, cubed	2–3 bayleaves
1 lb (450 g) pie veal, cubed	¼ level teaspoon whole allspice
8 oz (225 g) lamb kidneys	berries
4 carrots, peeled	¼ pt (150 ml) beef stock
6 small onions, peeled	2 tablespoons chopped parsley
salt and pepper	*Serves 4–5*

1 Place the pork and veal in a shallow ovenproof dish.

2 Remove the skin from the kidneys, cut out the core with a pair of scissors, cut each kidney into four. Add to the meat.

3 Cut the carrots into 1 inch (2 cm) slices, add to the meat with the whole onions.

4 Mix well and add salt, pepper, bayleaves, allspice and the stock which should only come halfway up the meat.

5 Cook uncovered in a moderate oven 350°F (180°C), gas mark 4 for 2½ hours stirring occasionally.

6 Serve sprinkled with the chopped parsley.

●
Köyhät Ritarit
Poor knights

One of the compensations of the short summer is the profusion of berries to end a meal – wild strawberries, raspberries, cranberries, orange-yellow cloudberries and garnet-coloured lingonberries. Hours are spent jam-making and converting wild fruit into alcoholic drinks. Here is a typically Finnish summer sweet.

2 eggs	1 lb (450 g) fresh strawberries, sliced
8 fl oz (250 ml) milk	
pinch of cinnamon	$\frac{1}{2}$ pint (300 ml) whipping cream whipped and slightly sweetened
1 teaspoon vanilla essence	
4 slices of bread	caster sugar to dredge (optional)
2 oz (50 g) unsalted butter	*Serves 4*

1 Break the eggs into a shallow dish, add the milk, cinnamon and vanilla essence, beat well to break up the egg.

2 Dip the bread slices in the egg, turning them to soak both sides.

3 Fry in the melted butter to brown each side lightly.

4 Place the fried bread diagonally down the centre of a serving dish, put a thick row of unsweetened strawberries down the centre.

5 Fill a piping bag with the whipped cream and pipe down each side of the berries in a simple design.

6 If liked, sprinkle generously with caster sugar.

Germany

Germany has an unfair reputation for stolid fare – plates heaped as high as an Alp. But it is not all potatoes, sausages, dumplings, schnitzels and sauerkraut. By the nineteenth century German food was a comfortable combination of peasant fare and the French-influenced diet of the wealthy burghers.

Sweet paprika, caraway seeds, juniper berries, allspice, cinnamon, cloves, dill and pepper have always played a big part in flavouring food. Other typical ingredients are almonds, apples, vinegar, sour cream and onions. Although potatoes, introduced in the eighteenth century by Frederick the Great, are still popular, consumption has dropped by almost half in the last fifty years.

One of Germany's great chefs is Helmut Abrell, who cooks at the Hotel Hirsch in Bad Wurzach, a spa a hundred kilometres west of Munich. The recipes he feels comfortable with are old and traditional. 'To be a chef,' he says, 'one must know the tradition of the recipes to be prepared, and one must be natural and confident in cooking them. You must taste often what you are cooking, just like a painter who must see colours or a musician who must hear sounds.'

Schwäbische Maultaschen
Meat dumplings

A native of Swabia, Chef Abrell enjoys preparing noodle dishes.

Schwäbische Maultaschen are very much like Italian ravioli or Chinese won-tons – filled pouches of dough. For this recipe Abrell uses pork, but chicken and beef can be substituted.

Filling	hot stock
8 oz (225 g) fresh spinach	
8 oz (225 g) pork (chicken or beef)	**Pastry**
$\frac{1}{2}$ level teaspoon pepper	10 oz (275 g) plain white flour
$\frac{1}{2}$ level teaspoon ground mace	$\frac{1}{4}$ level teaspoon salt
$\frac{1}{2}$ level teaspoon marjoram	2 large eggs
2 oz (50 g) white bread	2 egg yolks
2 oz (50 g) butter	2 tablespoons oil
2 oz (50 g) onion, chopped	a little beaten egg
1 level tablespoon chopped parsley	
1 thin slice lemon peel	
2 anchovy fillets	
salt	*Serves 4–6* (Makes 32)

1 Cook spinach in boiling salted water for a few minutes, drain and refresh in cold water, then squeeze well.

2 Cut pork into pieces and mix with mace and marjoram.

3 Add the spinach to the pork.

4 Melt the butter, add the onion and cook for a few minutes to soften. Add the parsley.

5 Mix the remaining filling ingredients into the pork and either mince or put in a food processor. Add salt and extra pepper if necessary.

For the pastry:
6 Combine the flour, salt, eggs and yolks (beaten together), then add the oil and mix to a pliable dough. Cover and leave to stand at room temperature for $\frac{1}{2}$ hour.

7 Roll out the pastry to approximately 16 × 20 inches (41 × 51 cm), and brush egg in four strips on the pastry beginning with an unbrushed strip, then egg-brushed, then unbrushed and so on.

8 Divide the filling into 4 portions and spread 1 portion along the first unbrushed strip.

9 Begin rolling up the pastry in swiss-roll fashion until the first roll of filling has been enclosed and the egg-brushed strip has been covered. Seal well and cut down the length with a pastry wheel, if available (this helps to seal the edges).

10 Continue in this way until there are four complete rolls.

11 Using the back of a knife, press each roll into eight, so that each cut edge is sealed, then cut with a pastry wheel or knife to completely enclose the filling like a ravioli dumpling.

12 Cook in batches in hot stock for 15 minutes, turning them over as necessary.

13 Serve with chopped onion fried in butter and fresh chopped chives sprinkled over.

Perch Stuffed with Pike

Because Bad Wurzach is a long way from the sea, the fish that
form so fundamental a part of Helmut Abrell's menus are
freshwater – pike, perch, trout and carp and all very easy to
get hold of. 'I always try to buy the freshest fish possible and
use it the same day. Freshwater fish should have no odour.
They should have bright, not sunken, eyes. The skin should
be smooth, the body not soft but firm, and the gills red or
rose-coloured.'

This dish is perch stuffed with pike. Abrell created it to
honour the opening of a friend's restaurant. 'Though it is a
new dish,' he says, 'its ingredients are from nearby and have
been used for years. The dish itself didn't just happen, it
evolved over a long period. In fact every time I prepare fish, I
use it as an opportunity to devise a new sauce or garnish. Here
I take advantage of the crayfish shells to make a bisque-like
sauce. Why not try to create something yourself? I think that's
the real fun of cooking, doing something on your own without
the aid of a cookery book or a teacher.'

Pike filling	To cook the crayfish
1 large pike, skinned and filleted to give 1 lb (450 g) fish	4 or 8 crayfish
	1 small carrot, sliced
a little salt	1 small onion, sliced
$\frac{1}{8}$ teaspoon cayenne pepper	1 level teaspoon caraway seeds
1 egg white	salt
4 fl oz (100 ml) single cream	$1\frac{1}{2}$ oz (40 g) butter
4 medium sized perch or 8 small perch, skinned and filleted	6 oz (175 g) onion, chopped
	4 fl oz (100 ml) dry white wine
Sauce	4 tablespoons oil
$1\frac{1}{2}$ oz (40 g) butter	2 fl oz (50 ml) brandy, optional
1 medium sized spring onion, chopped	4 fl oz (100 ml) white wine
	Garnish
$\frac{1}{2}$ pint (300 ml) single cream	Tomatoes skinned and seeds removed
pepper and cayenne	
2 level teaspoons arrowroot	Diced cucumber
1 tablespoon liquor from the cooked perch	*Serves 4 as a main course or 8 as a starter*

1 Cut the pike fillets into pieces, either mince or put through a food processor with the salt and cayenne until there is a paste consistency.

2 Place mixture in a bowl over another bowl filled with ice cubes. Gradually beat in the egg white and the cream. This helps to keep the filling firm and fresh.

3 Spread the filling over half of the skinned perch fillets. Cover with the remaining fillets to make sandwiches.

4 Meanwhile, cook the crayfish in $1\frac{1}{2}$ pints (850 ml) of boiling water with the sliced onion, carrot, caraway and salt for about 8 minutes. Strain the stock and reserve 12 fl oz (375 ml).

5 Carefully remove the flesh from the crayfish, reserving both shells and the flesh.

6 Place the perch fillets in a shallow pan, so that the fish is in a single layer with $1\frac{1}{2}$ oz (40 g) butter, 2 oz (50 g) of the chopped onion and 4 fl oz (100 ml) of white wine. Cover and poach gently for 3–5 minutes each side depending on size.

7 Remove and place in a heated serving dish with crayfish meat arranged on top. Cover and keep warm. Reserve 1 tablespoon of the liquor.

8 Heat the oil in a pan with the remaining 4 oz (125 g) onion, reserved crayfish shells, brandy, if using, and white wine.

9 Simmer gently for 5 minutes to cook off the alcohol and reduce. Add crayfish stock, then strain and reserve liquor.

To make the sauce
10 Sauté the spring onion with the butter for a few seconds to soften. Pour in the cream, keeping the pan on a very low heat.

11 Blend the arrowroot with the reserved crayfish stock, and add to the cream with salt and pepper and 1 tablespoon of the liquor the perch was cooked in.

12 Heat gently, stirring until the sauce thickens. If cooked too quickly the sauce will curdle slightly, but it will still taste all right.

13 Pour over the fish and, if liked, garnish with tomato and cucumber dice which have been previously heated in a little butter.

Peach Sherbet

Quite often when Helmut Abrell cooks an elaborate meal, he will serve a sherbet between the courses to clear the palate. Sherbet, or sorbet, can also be used as a refreshingly light dessert at the end of a meal. If you don't have an electric ice-cream maker you can freeze the mixture in ice-cube trays, so long as you beat it several times during the freezing process.

6 large fresh peaches	8 fl oz (225 ml) boiling water
juice 2 lemons	very dry champagne
4 oz (125 g) granulated sugar	*Serves 6*

1 Place peaches in boiling water for 20 seconds, then quickly into iced water. Peel off the skins.

2 Remove the stones, purée the flesh with the lemon juice to give ½ pint (300 ml) of purée.

3 Dissolve the sugar in the 8 fl oz (225 ml) boiling water, stir into the purée and place the mixture in an ice-cream machine. Alternatively place in a plastic container and put in the freezer or ice-making compartment of your refrigerator. Whisk several times during the freezing process.

4 Spoon into glasses and, if liked, pour a little champagne into each glass.

Redcurrant Pie

Along with the Viennese, the Germans are usually regarded as the great bakers of Europe. 'We Germans love sweet things,' Helmut admits, 'and the number of desserts we can offer is staggering. We say *Kein Meister ist vom Himmel gefallen* – experts don't fall out of the sky. I'm always learning, from colleagues, from customers, from experience. After all, cooking is an art form that can't be mechanical. It cannot be perfected without imagination, understanding and dedication.'

This is a delicious pudding with a very special and quite delicate flavour. As well as redcurrants, fresh blackcurrants or white currants could be used. Frozen currants can be used but need to be thawed slightly first, as they may sink in the meringue.

Pastry	4 egg whites
8 oz (225 g) plain flour	4 oz (125 g) caster sugar
1 oz (25 g) caster sugar	3 oz (75 g) ground almonds
4 oz (125 g) softened butter	12 oz (375 g) redcurrants
½ small egg	icing sugar to dredge
1 tablespoon milk	whipped cream
Filling	
1 oz (25 g) digestive biscuits, crushed	*Serves 6–8*

1 Combine flour, sugar and butter together. Add the egg and milk and mix to a dough. Wrap in cling film and chill for 1 hour.

2 Roll out pastry to line the base and sides of a 9 inch (23 cm) spring form cake tin.

3 Sprinkle the biscuits on the pastry base.

4 Whisk the egg whites until stiff, gradually whisk in the sugar a spoonful at a time. Add the ground almonds and redcurrants and gently fold in.

5 Turn mixture into pastry case, spread evenly.

6 Bake at 400°F (200°C), gas mark 6 for 20 minutes, reduce oven temperature to 350°F (180°C), gas mark 4 for 15–20 minutes until the top is light brown.

7 Dredge with icing sugar and serve hot or cold with whipped cream.

*F*rance

In France, regional dishes have survived despite the rising tide of what might be called *'le convenience'* and the asperities of *nouvelle cuisine*. The following recipes come from the Dauphiné, an upland region which has given its name to *pommes de terre dauphinoise*.

Up in the mountains there are wild truffles, morels and *cèpes*, local honey, plenty of freshwater fish and game, walnuts, hazelnuts and a cheese called *reblechon*. There is also an old inn in La Vallée de Desert called the Auberge de l'Âtre Fleuri near Saint-Pierre de Chartreuse. The inn is owned by André Revest who was born in La Cadière d'Azur in Provence. He began his professional life at the age of 14 as an apprentice in a restaurant at Hendaye on the Spanish border.

'My grandfather,' he says, 'was a marvellous chef and he taught me two simple secrets of great cooking: always buy fresh and always buy what is in season. Now that I am a chef this has become my basic philosophy.'

Truite à la Pâte d'Amandes
Trout with almond paste

Since the province of Dauphiné is famous for its fish, André Revest often prepares *truite à la pâte d'amandes*. He keeps the trout from a local stream alive in a freshwater tank until just before he cooks them.

	Almond paste
4 large rainbow trout, cleaned	**Almond paste**
2 tablespoons oil	3 oz (75 g) butter
1 oz (25 g) butter	8 oz (225 g) ground almonds
pinch of salt and pepper	juice 1 lemon
	large pinch of salt
	freshly ground white pepper
	Serves 4

1 Heat the oil and butter in a large frying pan, add salt and pepper. Add the fish.

2 Fry gently turning once after 3 minutes, shaking the pan to prevent the fish from sticking.

3 Remove onto an oval ovenproof dish and keep on one side.

4 Prepare the almond paste by melting the butter in a pan, add the ground almonds, lemon juice, salt and pepper and stir over a medium heat.

5 Fill the cavity of each trout with half the paste.

6 Spoon the remaining paste on top of each fish.

7 Bake in a hot oven 450°F (230°C), gas mark 8 for 10 minutes until the almond paste is golden and forms a light crust.

Tomates à la Provençale
Provençal tomatoes

Another speciality that André Revest serves is *tomates à la provençale*. This dish is typical of the cooking of southern France, combining tomatoes and *persillade* – chopped parsley and garlic. 'I cannot imagine cooking without garlic,' André says, 'or the beautiful tomatoes of the south. These have the sweet flavour of the earth.'

4 medium sized tomatoes cut in half cross-wise	4 cloves garlic, crushed
	1 oz (25 g) fresh breadcrumbs
salt and pepper	2–3 tablespoons olive oil
2 oz (50 g) freshly chopped parsley	*Serves 4*

1 Place the tomatoes in an ovenproof dish, season with salt and pepper.

2 Mix the parsley and garlic together, place on each tomato.

3 Sprinkle each with breadcrumbs and a few drops of oil.

4 Add a little water to the dish to prevent the tomatoes sticking.

5 Bake in a hot oven 450°F (230°C), gas mark 8 for 10–15 minutes.

Gratin Dauphinois
Casserole of potatoes in cream

'Gratin' means a crust and *gratin dauphinois* is the famous crusted potato casserole now found all over the world. The dish is flavoured with André Revest's special herb mixture: equal parts of thyme, oregano and rosemary, herbs he gets from his father's farm in Provence. Rosemary grows along the coast of the Mediterranean. *Romarin* in French, its Latin translation is 'dew of the sea'.

2 lb (1 kg) new potatoes, peeled and cut into thin slices	salt and pepper
	½ oz (15 g) butter
1½ pints (845 ml) milk	½ pint (275 ml) double cream, lightly whipped
4 cloves garlic, crushed	
1 teaspoon each of chopped fresh oregano, thyme and rosemary	6 oz (175 g) gruyère cheese, grated
	Serves 4–6

1 Bring the milk to the boil in a saucepan, add the garlic, herbs, salt and pepper.

2 Add the potatoes and allow to simmer, stirring occasionally to prevent the potatoes sticking to the bottom of the pan, and cook for about 20 minutes until just tender without breaking up.

3 Butter a flameproof dish and lift the potatoes out of the milk with a draining spoon into the dish.

4 Spoon the cream over and sprinkle with the cheese.

5 Place dish under a hot grill until the cheese has melted and is golden brown.

●

Champignons à la Provençale
Provençal mushrooms

In France, vegetables are taken very seriously. 'They are not thought of as simply garnishes to be thrown on a plate alongside meat and potatoes. I give them as much attention as the meat course I will cook later, because to me, as to all serious chefs, every part of a meal is important,' says André Revest.

When you come to choose mushrooms for *champignons à la provençale* remember that 'the size of a mushroom is no indication of its ripeness or its age; a small one can be as ripe as a large one. Nero called them food fit for the gods – believe me, prepared in the style of Provence, they are!'

1 lb (450 g) button mushrooms	2 oz (50 g) freshly chopped parsley
2 tablespoons olive oil	4 cloves garlic, crushed
2 oz (50 g) butter	salt and pepper
2 fl oz (50 ml) white wine	*Serves 4–6*

1 Wash the mushrooms and drain well.

2 Heat the oil and butter in a saucepan, add the mushrooms and sauté over a high heat for 2–3 minutes.

3 Add the wine and cook over a high heat until completely evaporated.

4 Stir in the parsley, garlic, salt and pepper and serve at once.

●

Selle d'Agneau
Lamb chops

One of the most striking features of André Revest's inn is its large open hearth where a pile of huge beech and pine logs crackle and roar on a firebrick platform. He cooks a lot of his meat on the embers of this fire. Lamb will cook for only five minutes on each side; the French like their beef rare and their lamb pink.

4 loin of lamb chops	1 tablespoon fresh chopped herbs, thyme, rosemary, oregano
salt and pepper	
	Serves 4

1 Season the chops by rubbing in salt, pepper and herbs.

2 Place under a pre-heated grill for 10 minutes, turning once, so that the meat is still slightly pink.

●

La Neige à la Liqueur Chartreuse
Soufflé with Chartreuse liqueur

As a final course André Revest may prepare a dessert using the local liqueur of the Carthusian monks, Chartreuse. 'A meal,' he says, 'should grow from course to course and the dessert should always be a pleasant surprise.'

There are two kinds of Chartreuse, green which is known as *Chartreuse de santé*, a liqueur believed to have health-giving properties, and the yellow, which is sweeter and contains less alcohol. The liqueur is made in Italy and Spain too but its formula, which involves a wide variety of herbs and plants, is secret. When making *la neige à la liqueur* be careful to fold the egg whites into the yolk mixture delicately. 'You have to be careful not to break the whites or this wonderful dessert will fall flat when it is cooked. As I place it on the plate, I see myself, for a moment, as a sculptor working in clay, making shapes like the mountains that surround the valley. The secret is to cook it quickly at a high temperature, so that the liqueur won't evaporate,' says André Revest.

4 egg yolks	1 oz (25 g) unsalted butter
8 egg whites	1 oz (25 g) icing sugar
4 oz (125 g) caster sugar	
6 tablespoons green Chartreuse	*Serves 4–6*

1 Place the yolks in a bowl with the caster sugar and beat until thick, pale and creamy.

2 Add 4 tablespoons of the Chartreuse, mix well and keep on one side.

3 Butter a flat oval ovenproof dish and coat with the icing sugar.

4 Whisk the egg whites until really stiff and dry.

5 Gently fold one third of the whites into the yolk mixture to lighten the yolks. Add this to the remaining egg whites, fold lightly without losing any volume.

6 Transfer the mixture to the prepared dish and leave in craggy heaps to represent the mountains.

7 Bake in a pre-heated hot oven 400°F (200°C), gas mark 6 for 8–10 minutes to lightly brown.

8 Spoon the remaining Chartreuse over the top and ignite. Serve at once.

Note Grand Marnier can be substituted for the Chartreuse if not available.

The Netherlands

In their low-lying country facing the North Sea, the Dutch specialise in substantial and nourishing food, much of it designed to keep the cold out. Chef Hans Clemens' heart belongs to the flat, wet, and windy Dutch countryside. Like most Netherlanders, he grew up on a small farm where hard work and good food were a way of life. While times are not as difficult as in the past, the simple, nutritious and filling dishes of the countryside are still very much a part of his cooking. 'My career,' he says, 'began more than 25 years ago right here at the Hotel Krasnapolsky. I have worked in many hotels in Europe and America, but decided to come home to do what I love best – Dutch cooking.'

Gevrulde Tomaat met Garnalen
Tomatoes filled with prawns

Dutch meals usually begin with a fish course and Hans Clemens has chosen to start with a variation on prawn cocktail. Chef Clemens insists on using fresh North Sea prawns, but frozen ones make an acceptable substitute.

A very simple and effective starter for a meal, the presentation is typical of the Dutch in trying to depict a still-life painting to give their culinary skills a touch of art.

4 oz (125 g) peeled prawns	4 small tomatoes
2 teaspoons mayonnaise	Garnish – celery, watercress and
1 tablespoon chopped parsley	lemon slices
salt and pepper	*Serves 2*

1 Drain the prawns well on kitchen paper.

2 In a bowl, mix the prawns, mayonnaise, parsley, salt and pepper.

3 Cut a small piece off the rounded end of the tomatoes and scoop out the flesh with a teaspoon. (This can be used in a soup or a stew).

4 Fill the hollowed-out tomatoes with the prawn mixture.

5 Arrange 2 tomatoes on each plate side by side and replace the tomato 'lids'.

6 Decorate the plates with celery leaves and stalks to give a tulip effect, watercress and the lemon slices in twists.

Ertwensoep
Pea soup

There are as many varieties of *ertwensoep* in Holland as there are chefs. 'The Dutch love this dried pea soup, but it's not made all the year round. As soon as the cold weather sets in, signs go up in restaurants, hotels and cafés announcing the arrival of *ertwensoep*. What gives my recipe its special flavour are the different pieces of pork that I put into it,' says Hans Clemens. The soup is a meal in itself. According to connoisseurs it should be so thick that a spoon can stand in it unsupported.

'There's nothing better than *ertwensoep* on a cold, raw day. After working outside, biking or skating, wouldn't you love to come into the kitchen to these aromas? It's the perfect Dutch dish . . . simple, solid nourishment with no fancy trimmings and if you can't finish it all today, it will be just as good reheated tomorrow – better perhaps.'

1 lb (450 g) dried peas	8 oz (225 g) lean belly of pork, rind removed
1 pig's knuckle cut in half (this is the trotter and part of the leg with meat on; obtainable from a good butcher)	salt and pepper
	2 tablespoons chopped parsley
	1 Dutch smoked sausage ring, cut into ½ inch (1 cm) pieces
6 oz (175 g) onion, chopped	
1 large leek, diced	
2 sticks celery, chopped	*Serves 4–6*

1 Soak the peas overnight in 2½ pints (1½ litres) of water. Then simmer them in the soaking water for about 3 hours until tender. Skim off any scum that forms.

2 Meanwhile, cook the pig's knuckle in water for about 2 hours to give 1¾ pints (1 litre) stock.

3 Add the stock, onion, leek, celery and belly of pork cut in pieces to the peas and cook for 1–1½ hours, so that the flavours can mingle.

4 Remove the meat from the knuckle and cut in pieces. Add to the peas with salt, pepper, parsley and the sausage, and simmer long enough for the sausage to heat through.

5 Serve with pumpernickel bread and thickly sliced boiled bacon.

●

Kip Grootmoedersstyl
Grandmother's chicken casserole

'Years ago,' says Chef Clemens, 'in my grandmother's day most people didn't have ovens, only top burners, and that's why a large pot is called a Dutch oven. *Kip grootmoedersstyl* is one of my favourite recipes. When I was a child I watched my grandmother make this dish many times. Maybe it was then that I decided to be a chef. It looks good, tastes delicious, and makes a really nourishing and filling main course.'

1½ oz (40 g) butter	6 oz (175 g) parboiled small potatoes
two 2–2½ lb (1 kg) approx. chickens	6 oz (175 g) parboiled carrots
salt and pepper	6 oz (175 g) mushrooms, washed
4 oz (125 g) onions, chopped	4 oz (125 g) frozen peas, thawed
6 oz (175 g) smoked streaky bacon, chopped	*Serves 4*

1 Melt the butter in a large, wide, flameproof casserole.

2 Remove giblets from the chickens and season the birds inside with salt and pepper.

3 Place in the pan and quickly brown both sides of the chickens.

4 Put the casserole in a pre-heated oven 350°F (180°C), gas mark 4, uncovered, for about 40 minutes until the chickens are tender.

5 Remove the chickens and keep on one side.

6 Add the onion and bacon to the pan and cook over a moderate heat to soften the onion.

7 Add the potatoes, carrots and mushrooms to the pan and heat gently.

8 Meanwhile, carefully cut the chickens in half along the breastbone, remove the backbone and place chickens in a serving dish and keep hot.

9 Add the peas, cook gently just to heat through as the peas should not be mushy.

10 Adjust seasoning and spoon the vegetables over the chickens with some of the pan juices, if liked.

●

Bloemkool met Kassaus
Cauliflower with creamy Gouda sauce

Cheese is of central importance in the Dutch diet. The three classic cheeses are still made, sometimes in the old-fashioned way, on farms near the towns whose names they bear: Edam, Leiden and Gouda. Edam is a yellow, mellow-flavoured, semi-soft cheese made partially from skimmed milk. Leiden cheese, flavoured with caraway and cumin seeds, has a firmer texture. Gouda is made of whole milk and is formed in the shape of a wheel. Although the Dutch love cheese, they haven't created many original cheese dishes. They like to pour cheese sauces over their vegetables, and this is a Dutch version of a basic bechamel with extra ingredients.

1 head cauliflower, trimmed	2 egg yolks
1½ oz (40 g) butter or margarine	6 oz (175 g) Gouda cheese
1½ oz (40 g) plain flour	salt and pepper
½ pint (300 ml) milk	*Serves 3–4*

1 Cook the cauliflower in boiling salted water until just tender (10 minutes). Remove with slotted spoon to a serving dish.

2 Melt the butter or margarine in a saucepan over a low heat. Stir in the flour and cook for 1 minute.

3 Gradually beat in the milk until there are no lumps.

4 Carefully add the egg yolks one at a time, stirring continuously over a *low* heat to thicken the sauce.

5 Stir in most of the Gouda. Heat to melt the cheese and give a smooth sauce, then pour over the cauliflower having seasoned to taste.

6 Sprinkle remaining cheese on top; either place under a pre-heated grill to brown lightly or put in the oven 350°F (180°C), gas mark 4 for 10 minutes.

Dutch Apple Pie

In the kitchens of the Hotel Krasnapolsky, Chef Jan Hals has created a prize-winning recipe for a sweet, rich Dutch apple pie. Apple pie is the traditional dessert eaten throughout December, starting during the first week, on St Nikolaas night.

Pastry	Filling	
4 oz (100 g) butter, softened	6 oz (175 g) seedless raisins	
8 oz (225 g) caster sugar	2 lb (1 kg) cooking apples	
12 oz (375 g) plain flour	2 tablespoons lemon juice	
2 eggs (size 4) beaten	2 oz (50 g) caster sugar	
	1 level tablespoon ground cinnamon	
	1 oz (25 g) fresh breadcrumbs	
	Serves 6–8	

1 Place the butter on a pastry board, soften with the fingertips and work in the sugar.

2 Gradually work in the flour and then the eggs. Knead together to form a dough. Wrap in cling-film and chill for 30 minutes.

3 Meanwhile, pour boiling water over the raisins to soften and swell them.

4 Peel the apples and cut into dice, mix with the lemon juice.

5 Mix the caster sugar and cinnamon together, and stir into the apples with the drained raisins.

6 Lightly butter and flour a 9 inch (23 cm) spring-form cake tin. Cut off just less than one third of the pastry. Roll out the larger piece and use it to line the base and sides of the tin.

7 Sprinkle the breadcrumbs over the base of the tin and pour in the apple mixture.

8 Roll out the remaining pastry, cut into narrow strips and arrange on top of the pie to make a lattice.

9 Bake in a pre-heated oven 350°F (180°C), gas mark 4 for 35–40 minutes until just golden brown.

*I*taly

The Italians say '*a tavola non s'invecchia*' – at the table you never grow old, and in Venice, where this menu comes from, they make an art out of eating. The city itself was founded on the sea route which led down the Adriatic to Alexandria, thence to Cairo and far beyond to Ceylon, southern India and the Spice islands. Venetian merchants founded their wealth on the lucrative spice trade. By the fifteenth century Venetian cooking was renowned throughout Europe. It was the Venetians who were the first to bring glassware to the table and introduced that new-fangled and unheard-of novelty – the fork. The banquets of the Doges of Venice were the most elaborate and costly ever created.

Today, Venetian cooking is more restrained; a cuisine based on olives and olive oil, garlic, sweet basil, fennel, rosemary, thyme and cheeses. Chef Giovanni Niero runs the kitchen of a restaurant just outside Venice called *Al Postiglione*, and what follows is a typical meal you could choose from the fairly expansive menu.

●

Sauces

The basis for many of the dishes served at *Al Postiglione* is a sauce. 'It is we Italians,' says Niero, 'who truly developed the art of making sauce, not our French brothers, as so many believe. To us, sauces are not window-dressing but the very heart of certain dishes.' He will tell you that the Italian word for sauce, *salsa*, is derived from the Roman word for salt, *sal*, and that thickening a sauce with flour was a technique developed in Italy and which their cooks took to France.

The two most important sauces are *bolognese*, also called *ragu*, and *besciamella* or *salsa balsamella*, a basic white sauce with scores of uses. According to Niero, who is a bit of a patriot: 'It existed in Italy long before the time of Louis XIV, when it was named for Louis de Bechameil, the Marquis de Nointel.'

When making it, follow Niero's advice: 'It is traditional always to stir at an even speed and in the same direction. Some do, some don't, but whatever is done, there must be no lumps in the sauce. Use a heavy saucepan and a low steady heat, so that the sauce can thicken without burning.'

Bolognese Sauce

4 oz (125 g) onion, peeled	½ level teaspoon freshly ground pepper
4 oz (125 g) carrots, peeled	
1 stick celery, washed	½ pint (275 ml) red wine
8 oz (225 g) lean stewing beef	2 level tablespoons flour
8 oz (225 g) pork or veal	14 oz (400 g) can chopped tomatoes
2 tablespoons oil	½ pint (275 ml) beef stock
1 oz (25 g) butter	
pinch of salt	*Serves 4*

1 Mince or process the onion, carrots, celery, beef and pork or veal.

2 Place the oil and butter in a saucepan, add the minced vegetables and meat and cook for about 5 minutes.

3 Stir in the salt, pepper and wine, and cook until the wine has almost evaporated.

4 Stir in the flour, cook for 2 minutes, then add the tomatoes and stock.

5 Allow to simmer and thicken for 30 minutes, stirring occasionally.

Besciamella Sauce
Basic white sauce

To give a more savoury flavour to this sauce, warm the milk in a pan with a little onion, bayleaf, cloves and mace. Strain before using. This is then called bechamel sauce.

1 oz (25 g) butter	8 fl oz (225 ml) milk, at room temperature
1 oz (25 g) flour	
	salt and pepper

1 In a heavy saucepan melt the butter and blend in the flour over a low heat.

2 Gradually blend in the milk, then whisk until the sauce is smooth, bring to the boil and simmer for 2 minutes, whisking occasionally. Add salt and pepper to taste.

●
Tagliolini Verdi Gratinati

Pasta, which means dough or paste, is taken in one form or another in almost every Italian meal. Marco Polo is supposed to have brought pasta back from China, but modern research proves that the Italians were eating pasta long before he left for Cathay.

Pasta comes in many shapes and sizes – there are over 50 varieties. For *tagliolini verdi gratinati* fresh pasta, coloured and flavoured with spinach, is used. The word comes from *tagliare* which means to cut, and the *tagliolini* are actually cut from rolled sheets of dough made with wheat and eggs.

For perfectly cooked pasta use a large pot and lots of rapidly boiling water. Fresh pasta, if you can buy it, only takes two or three minutes of cooking before it becomes what the Italians call *al dente*, soft but still with a bit of bite in it.

1 lb (450 g) spinach noodles	1 recipe bechamel or basic white sauce
2 oz (50 g) butter, melted	
1 recipe bolognese sauce	freshly grated Parmesan cheese
	Serves 4

1 Cook noodles according to the directions on the packet. Drain well, and return to the same hot saucepan.

2 Add 2 tablespoons of the butter, the bolognese sauce and nearly all the bechamel, reserving approximately 4 tablespoons.

3 Mix together over a low heat and pour into a warm serving dish.

4 Top with the remaining sauce, sprinkle liberally with cheese and the remaining butter, place in a hot oven 400°F (200°C), gas mark 6 for about 10 minutes.

● Scampi alla Carlina

This next dish is built round a small delicacy from the Adriatic which is so closely associated with Venice that all over the world it is known by the Italian name. One of these morsels is called a *scampo*; when two or more are gathered together in a cocktail or in batter, they are *scampi*. *Scampi alla Carlina* is named after the sister of *Al Postiglione*'s manager. It was she who had the bright idea of adding gherkins and capers to the scampi.

1 lb (450 g) frozen peeled scampi, thawed	4 gherkins, chopped
	1 teaspoon capers, chopped
salt and pepper	juice of $\frac{1}{2}$ lemon
flour for dredging	10 drops of Worcestershire sauce
2 tablespoons oil	1 level tablespoon tomato purée
1 oz (25 g) butter, melted	*Serves 3–4*

1 Drain the scampi well on kitchen paper.

2 Toss the scampi in seasoned flour.

3 Heat the oil in a frying pan, add the scampi and cook to brown lightly for 5 minutes over a moderate heat to prevent the scampi from shrinking.

4 Place the scampi in a heated serving dish. Keep hot.

5 Add the butter to the pan with the remaining ingredients, stir and heat through; pour over the scampi and serve immediately.

Risi e Bisi
Venetian risotto

The next dish, *risi e bisi*, dates back to the early days of Venice. Basically a poor man's dish, it is said to have been served to the Doges of Venice to celebrate the feast of St Mark. Rice was introduced to Italy in the fifteenth century, and before long the Po valley became the major rice-growing region in Europe. That is why rice rivals pasta and bread as a staple of the diet in northern Italy. It is important to use a rice which can absorb the maximum amount of liquid without becoming mushy. The important thing in making this risotto is to stir often and add more broth if needed. The rice should never dry out. At the end it should be cooked *al dente*, soft on the outside, firm inside. Enough liquid should remain for the rice to be bubbling. 'We call it,' Niero says, '*riso all'onconda*, rippling rice.' Ernest Hemingway, a friend of the Cipriani family who manage *Al Postiglione*, was a great fan of *risi e bisi*.

'You may not think that rice and peas sound like a tempting combination,' Niero says, 'but the way we present it here in Venice, it really does capture the freshness of the peas. It is truly a dish that should be served only when peas are in season – in Venice only in the Spring.

1 small onion, finely chopped	6 oz (175 g) Italian rice, half cooked and drained
2 lettuce leaves, finely sliced	
2 tablespoons oil	4 oz (125 g) Parmesan cheese
1 pint (600 ml) chicken stock	
12 oz (375 g) peas	*Serves 4*

1 Place the onion and lettuce in a pan with the oil, cook until the onion is soft, about 3 minutes, adding 3 tablespoons of stock.

2 Cook the peas in a separate pan with half the remaining stock for a few minutes, add to the onion with the liquor.

3 Stir in the half-cooked rice and remaining stock, cook for about 20 minutes, adding more stock if necessary.

4 Stir in the cheese, salt and pepper and serve at once. This should be more juicy than a risotto and more solid than a soup.

●

Fegato alla Veneziana con Polenta
Venetian liver with corn bread

Venice is built on a hundred and seventeen islands linked by four hundred bridges. In the sixteenth century a Venetian ship tied up on the Grand Canal after a journey from the New World with a hold full of maize. For some reason the Venetians thought it came from Turkey, a clearing house for new foods, and they named it *granoturco*, Turkish grain. This soon became a staple food of the poor. It is now known as *polenta* and every family in northern Italy has its copper *polenta* pot, the *paiolo*. Italians eat *polenta* in place of bread, and they take it with butter and cheese or sauces, or frequently toast and fry it.

Venetian liver with corn bread, *fegato alla Veneziana con polenta*, must be eaten immediately it is ready. To cook the *polenta*, Niero adds the coarse cornmeal 'slowly, slowly, *a pioggia*, like gentle rain' to the boiling, salted water. 'The best way to do this,' he suggests, 'is to grab the cornmeal in the fist and allow some to sift through the fingers in a thin, barely perceptible stream. The important thing is to prevent lumps from forming, since they are difficult to break up'.

Polenta	2 teaspoons salt
Prepare 2 hours before liver	a little butter
8 oz (225 g) cornmeal	
2¾ pints (1⅝ litres) water	*Serves 4–6*

1 Bring the water and salt to the boil in a large saucepan.

2 Slowly pour in cornmeal, whisking all the time to prevent any lumps forming.

3 Cook for 45 minutes, stirring often to prevent the mixture from sticking.

4 Pour into a buttered shallow dish and leave for at least 2 hours.

5 Then, cut into portions and heat in a warm oven while preparing the liver.

Liver	salt
1 lb (450 g) calves' liver	1 tablespoon parsley, finely
3 oz (75 g) butter	chopped
4 tablespoons oil	3 tablespoons stock
4 oz (125 g) onion, finely sliced	*Serves 4–6*

1 Cut the liver into thin slivers, removing membrane.

2 Melt 2 oz (50 g) of the butter in a large frying pan, add 3 tablespoons of the oil, add the onions and cook until soft but not browned.

3 When onions are nearly cooked, push to one side of the pan, add the remaining oil and liver.

4 Cook quickly over a high heat for 5–6 minutes. About 1 minute before the end of the cooking time add the remaining butter and a pinch of salt, the parsley and stock.

5 Serve with the warmed polenta.

Note Buy the cornmeal from a shop with a good turnover. If it is stale, it can ruin the dish.

Crespelli
Pancakes

It was the Venetians who introduced sugar into Europe, so blame them if you have bad teeth. They don't eat puddings every day, preferring fresh fruit or cheese as a dessert, but on Sundays and feast days and at a formal dinner a sweet will be served, maybe *crespelli*. These are pancakes filled with pastry cream. 'Crêpes,' says Niero, 'are found in some form in many countries. You'll find them in Renaissance cookery books as *crespelle* or *crespe*. Once again I must say that the idea of crêpes went from Italy to France, not the other way round!'

4 oz (125 g) flour, sieved	4 fl oz (100 ml) milk
pinch of salt	a little melted butter
2 eggs	caster sugar for sprinkling
2 egg whites	
4 fl oz (100 ml) Cointreau	*Makes 8–10 pancakes*

1 Place the flour and salt in a bowl, add the whole eggs and mix well.

2 Beat in the egg whites a little at a time, then add 1 tablespoon of the Cointreau and sufficient milk to give a pouring consistency.

3 Pour a little butter in a small omelette pan and enough batter to cover the base of the pan thinly.

4 Cook over a moderate heat until the top of the pancake looks a little dry, then turn over with a spatula to cook the second side.

5 Spread each crêpe with some pastry cream (see over) or jam, then fold in half and spread with a little more and fold again to give a triangle.

6 Arrange in a buttered flameproof dish and sprinkle liberally with caster sugar.

7 Place under a hot grill to melt and caramelise the sugar.

8 Pour over remaining Cointreau and ignite. Serve at once.

Pastry cream	1 egg yolk
1 oz (25 g) butter	$\frac{1}{4}$ pint (125 ml) milk
$\frac{1}{2}$ oz (15 g) caster sugar	$\frac{1}{4}$ teaspoon vanilla essence
1 oz (25 g) plain flour	

1 Melt the butter in a small saucepan, stir in the sugar and flour.

2 Beat the egg yolk and milk together, add to the pan and cook gently over a moderate heat, beating all the time, until the mixture is thick.

3 Remove pan, add the vanilla and beat well.

Mexico

When Cortez and the other conquistadors arrived in Mexico in 1519, they found the rich Indian cultures of the Mayas, Aztecs, Toltecs, Mixtecs and Zapotecs, and they superimposed their own Spanish heritage on the native customs and traditions. The Indian staple diet of maize, beans, tomatoes and chillies was modified over the years by European preferences, and the result today is a mix of the old and the new world.

Despite the fact that more than half the population have European blood in their veins, there is a national pride in Mexico's Indian heritage – the only place in the world to rival the antiquity of Indian farming is the Middle East.

Chef Joaquin Guzman, who has provided these Mexican recipes, began cooking when he was 16 years old. 'I always liked it. The incredible combination of tastes you could prepare fascinated me.' This is a typical meal that might be eaten by any Mexico City family.

Guacamole
Avocado dip

'*Guacamole* is an Indian word that means avocado mixture. It comes from the Aztec word *ahuacatl* and *molli* which means concoction. There are many varieties of this dip, each with different ingredients, but this is the classic version', says Guzman.

Traditionally, *guacamole* is made in a mortar with a pestle; a blender is never used since *guacamole* is not supposed to be smooth or creamy. A really good one should have a slightly coarse texture. 'Guacamole should be served as soon as it's prepared', says Guzman. 'It is so delicate that its flavour is quickly lost and its colour begins to darken very quickly.' Some people like a little sour cream on their *guacamole*.

2 oz (50 g) onion	2 large ripe avocados
4 oz (100 g) tomatoes, skinned and deseeded	salt and pepper
	2 teaspoons olive oil
1 level tablespoon chopped parsley	**Garnish**
4 pieces of serrano chilli or 2 oz (50 g) green pepper and 1 oz (25 g) chilli, seeded and finely chopped	finely sliced onion rings (optional)
	Serves 4

1 Finely chop the onion on a board, add the tomato, chopped parsley, chilli and green pepper.

2 Cut the avocados in half, remove stones, scoop out the flesh and add to the tomatoes, etc.

3 Coarsely chop ingredients and mix together, season with salt and pepper.

4 Turn mixture into serving dish, sprinkle over olive oil and garnish, if liked, with onion rings.

5 Serve with tortilla chips or crisps.

Sopa de Medula
Beef marrow soup

Soup plays an extremely important part in Mexican cooking, and few menus are without it. Mexican soups are special because they are extraordinary mixtures of Indian, Spanish and even French cooking. If you cannot get beef marrow, salt pork or bacon will do. 'In some parts of Mexico the soup includes the herb *epazote*, but parsley can be used instead,' says Joaquin Guzman.

1 tablespoon olive or corn oil	2 pints (1 litre 150 ml) chicken stock
2 tablespoons finely chopped fresh garlic	1 green chilli finely chopped
	1 bayleaf
2 oz (50 g) onion, chopped	2 tablespoons chopped parsley
2 carrots, peeled and finely chopped	salt and pepper
2 stalks celery, chopped	**Garnish**
1 large leek, chopped	tortilla chips (optional)
6 oz (175 g) beef marrow or piece of salt belly pork or bacon	*Serves 4*

1 Heat the oil in a large heavy pan, add the garlic, and fry gently for 1 minute.

2 Add the prepared onions, carrots, celery, leek and beef marrow (or the pork in one piece) with the stock and the chilli.

3 Stir the vegetables over a low heat, adding bayleaf, parsley, salt and pepper.

4 Bring to the boil and simmer for about 7 minutes or until the vegetables are just cooked to retain some of their texture.

5 Remove salt pork, if used, adjust seasoning to taste. Stir in parsley and, if available, tortilla chips or chipsticks.

Pollo en Manchamanteles
Chicken stewed with fruits

For his main dish Chef Guzman suggests a chicken dish, because poultry has long been a Mexican favourite. *Manchamanteles* is translated as 'the tablecloth stainer'. 'If this sauce gets on a tablecloth the stain may never come out and will be there forever to remind you of a good meal,' he explains. The stain comes from the chillies.

Sauce	
4 oz (100 g) onion, coarsely chopped	4 large chicken quarters
2 cloves garlic	2–3 tablespoons olive or corn oil
2 bayleaves	freshly ground black pepper
2 level tablespoons fresh chopped oregano or 1 level tablespoon dried oregano	4 oz (100 g) onion, sliced
	9 fl oz strong beer (e.g. Guinness)
1 level tablespoon fresh thyme or ½ level tablespoon dried thyme	2 level tablespoons granulated sugar
	½ pint (250 ml) chicken stock
6 chile mulatos and 4 chile anchos or 8 oz (225 g) assorted peppers and 4 fresh chillies, seeded and chopped	4 oz (100 g) button onions, peeled
	4 oz (100 g) courgettes, chopped
	12 oz (375 g) fresh pears, chopped
¾ pint (375 ml) water	8 oz (225 g) firm banana, peeled and sliced
	4 oz (100 g) fresh pineapple, chopped
	4 oz (100 g) frozen peas, thawed
	Serves 4

1 Place the onion, garlic, bayleaves, herbs, prepared chillies (and peppers, if using) into a saucepan with the water.

2 Bring to the boil, simmer very gently for about 15 minutes until vegetables are tender, remove bayleaves, sieve or liquidise to make a smooth sauce. Keep on one side.

3 Heat oil in a large shallow heavy pan and cook chicken on all sides until lightly browned.

4 Sprinkle with pepper, add the onion and pour over the beer.

5 Spoon the prepared sauce over the chicken and sprinkle with the sugar, pour over the stock and add the button onions.

6 Simmer gently until chicken is tender for about 35–40 minutes. Then add the chopped courgettes, pears, banana, pineapple and sprinkle over the peas. Heat through and serve at once.

●

Sopes de Chorizo con Papas
Tortillas with sausage and potatoes

Mexico's version of fast food is *enchiladas*. The base of this snack is the *tortilla* made from maize. *Tortillas* can be filled with all sorts of mouthwatering ingredients from fried pork and red chilli sauce to cheese and green chilli sauce. *Sopes* are very popular *antojitos* – appetisers. They are small tortillas filled with all sorts of different savouries. Here is one example.

8 oz (225 g) fine cornmeal	8 oz (225 g) Chorizo sausage
2 oz (50 g) plain flour	Cos lettuce
$\frac{1}{2}$ pint (275 ml) water, approx.	4 oz (113 g) cottage cheese
3 oz (75 g) lard	
1 lb (450 g) par-boiled potatoes, finely diced	*Serves 6*

1 Mix the cornmeal and flour in a bowl, stir in sufficient water to mix to a firm dough. Turn onto a well floured board, knead lightly, then roll out to about $\frac{1}{8}$ inch (0.5 cm) thick. Cut into twelve 3 inch (8 cm) rounds.

2 Pre-heat a large heavy frying pan or griddle, grease lightly and cook the tortillas until lightly browned on both sides.

3 Lift tortillas onto a heated serving dish and, using thumb and forefinger, pinch up the edges to form a rim. Keep warm on one side.

4 Melt the lard in a frying pan, pour about 1 teaspoon over each tortilla.

5 Add the diced potatoes and sausage to the pan and fry until heated through. Spoon this mixture onto the tortillas.

6 Garnish each with shredded lettuce and cottage cheese.

7 Just before serving, pour 1 tablespoon of *salsa verde* (see below) over each.

Note Chorizo sausage can be obtained in this country from good delicatessens but, if unavailable, use diced salami.

●

Salsa Verde
Green tomato sauce

12 oz (375 g) green tomatoes, chopped	2 tablespoons freshly chopped parsley
2 oz (50 g) onion, chopped	2 small green chillies
2 cloves garlic, chopped or crushed	salt and pepper

1 Place all the ingredients in a small saucepan and bring to the boil.

2 Simmer sauce gently until ingredients are soft. Beat well with a spoon to make a smooth sauce and season with salt and pepper.

Note If green tomatoes are unavailable, use fresh red or drained canned tomatoes.

Filete de Robalo Veracruzana
Sea bass Vera Cruz style

It is said that when Montezuma ruled in the fifteenth century he liked seafood so much that he had runners bring him fresh fish daily from the coastal city of Vera Cruz 200 miles away. Mexicans still love fish, and the Vera Cruz style is tomato sauce flavoured with olives and capers.

2 lb (1 kg) thick fillets sea bass (or fresh haddock) cut into four	**Sauce**
	2 tablespoons chopped garlic
Poaching liquid	3 tablespoons olive or corn oil
2 oz (50 g) onion, finely chopped	4 oz (125 g) green pepper
2 oz (50 g) carrots, chopped	4 oz (125 g) onion, chopped
2 oz (50 g) celery, chopped	2 lb (1 kg) tomatoes, skinned and deseeded
2 bayleaves	
1 sprig of thyme	4 oz (125 g) green olives
2 cloves garlic	salt and pepper
2 pints (1 litre 150 ml) water	2 tablespoons capers
	chopped parsley
	Serves 4

1 Combine all the ingredients for the poaching liquid in a large pan. The pan should be large enough to hold fish in a single layer.

2 Bring the stock to the boil and simmer for 10–15 minutes, then add the prepared fillets and cook for 1 minute to just cook the fish. Keep on one side.

3 Meanwhile, in another large pan, fry the garlic in the oil for about 1 minute. Add the prepared green pepper, onion, tomatoes and green olives.

4 Add ¼ pint (150 ml) of the poaching liquid to the vegetables, season with salt and pepper and cook gently for 5 minutes.

5 Lower the drained fish into the vegetables, add the capers and simmer for 2 minutes.

6 Garnish, if liked, with steamed potatoes and chopped parsley.

Dulce de Coco con Piña
Sweet coconut with pineapple

One of Chef Guzman's favourite desserts is *dulce de coco con piña*. 'The wonderful aroma of fresh Mexican pineapples can perfume a whole room,' he says.

1 fresh pineapple	4 oz (125 g) blanched whole almonds, coarsely chopped
8 oz (225 g) granulated sugar	
4 oz (125 g) fresh shredded coconut, or 3 oz (75 g) dried *shredded* coconut	3 oz (75 g) pecan nuts, coarsely chopped
	2 oz (50 g) unsalted butter
	Serves 4–6

1 Cut the base off the pineapple, place on a board and cut off the top. Reserve the leaves.

2 Using a sharp stainless knife, cut off the skin vertically, and chop the flesh finely.

3 Place the sugar in a large frying pan, add the pineapple, stir until sugar dissolves.

4 Add the coconut, nuts and butter. Cook very gently for 45 minutes stirring occasionally.

5 Pre-heat oven to 350°F (180°C), gas mark 4.

6 Turn the pineapple into a large shallow ovenproof dish and bake for 10 minutes. Serve either hot or cold decorated with extra pecans round the edge and the reserved leaves.

Hong Kong

Chef Leung Ting-Kee, known as T-K to his friends, originally came to Hong Kong from Canton, and he specialises in Cantonese dishes. His principal aid is the shallow heavy cooking bowl known as a wok – a chinese word for cooking vessel. It is ideal for quick-drying, stir-frying and deep-frying. If you don't own a wok, a heavy cast-iron pan will do instead.

Over the centuries the Chinese have developed a cuisine which tends to contrast the five basic flavours – sweet, sour, bitter, salty and hot. The Chinese like to buy all their ingredients as fresh as possible. Go to a market in Hong Kong and you'll find all the ducks and chickens alive, frogs hopping about in cages, carp swimming in water. Freshness is all.

The noticeable distinction of the Chinese kitchen is the way in which all the raw materials are prepared in advance. The chopping and slicing is only the prelude to cooking which takes place at great speed. Vegetables are never overcooked; plunged into the wok, the goodness is sealed-in at high speed. The beauty of the wok is that it retains its heat, and each successive operation can be done quickly without waiting for saucepans to come to the boil.

Some of the ingredients used in the Hong Kong and Japanese recipes may be difficult to find unless you go to a Chinese supermarket, but it is possible to substitute other things:

Mirin a Japanese sweet rice wine. There is no Chinese equivalent. It is difficult to find, and there are two qualities. Use a sweet wine or sherry as a substitute.

Sake a rice wine which comes normal or dry. Quite easy to find in Chinese shops or supermarkets. A medium dry or light-bodied sherry could be used instead.

Karashi mustard sold dry or made up in tubes. It is a strong mustard like the English variety rather than the French.

Rice vinegar easy to find in both Chinese and Japanese food shops.

Shikaki mushrooms large dried Japanese forest mushrooms. Very expensive and they need soaking before use.

Enoki small dried mushrooms, difficult to find.

Chinese dried mushrooms easily available from both Japanese and Chinese shops, but they are expensive.

Monosodium glutamate available in Chinese or Japanese shops, but you can buy monosodium glutamate flavour boosters in supermarkets (Aromat).

These comments are a guide for the Hong Kong and Japanese sections, but the main thing to remember is that the vegetables should usually be served slightly crisp.

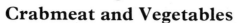

Crabmeat and Vegetables

Vegetables play a prominent part in Cantonese cooking. In eastern China there are seventeen different kinds of bean alone. European cooks are only now beginning to prepare their vegetables in the Chinese style – a minimum of cooking and a determination to retain colour, flavour and vitamins. In this dish the crabmeat is freshly steamed and the egg whites are used as a sealer to keep the shellfish from losing its juices in the wok. When T-K makes this dish, he cuts all his ingredients into small, uniform pieces which can easily be picked up with chopsticks. The knife and fork is never used at a Chinese dinner table. Apart from crab, the Chinese use prawns, shrimps, lobster, abalone, clams and scallops in their seafood dishes.

¾ pint (425 ml) chicken stock	1 teaspoon sugar
pinch of salt	1 lb (450 g) button mushrooms, wiped
5 tablespoons vegetable oil	
1 lb (450 g) broccoli, flowers and top part of stalk, cut into bite-size pieces	8 oz (225 g) cooked white crabmeat, flaked
	1 tablespoon sesame oil
2 tablespoons chinese rice wine or white wine	1 level tablespoon cornflour
	1 egg white, lightly beaten
¼ level teaspoon fresh grated ginger	*Serves 3–4*

1 Place the chicken stock, salt and 2 tablespoons of the vegetable oil in a wok or saucepan. Bring to the boil.

2 Add the broccoli, wine, ginger and sugar. Sauté for a few minutes until still crisp, lift out the broccoli with a slotted spoon, arrange on a dish and keep hot.

3 Add the mushrooms and another tablespoon of oil, bring the liquid back to the boil and cook briefly. Lift out with a slotted spoon and place on top of the broccoli. Keep hot.

4 Pour off the liquid from the wok, and wipe clean with kitchen paper.

5 Add the crabmeat to the wok with the remaining 2 tablespoons vegetable oil, add the sesame oil and the cornflour. Stir to heat quickly, add the egg white, stir for a few seconds.

6 Pour the crabmeat over the vegetables and serve.

●
Duck with Water Chestnuts

It is said that Chinese fishermen have been working at their nets for over fifty centuries. When it comes to Chinese cooking, you really are confronted with a culture so ancient that it makes the glories of Greece and Rome look transient. In artistry and invention their civilisation has never been surpassed; their food is a reflection of a long heritage of expertise.

This dish uses both soy sauce and oyster sauce. Soy sauce is a fermented extract of the soya bean, chief among the many sauces to be found in a Chinese kitchen. The beauty of this dish is that the vegetables are suffused with the flavour of the duck. All over China ducks are farmed, frequently alongside the same ponds in which freshwater carp are being reared. After pork, fish and poultry are the foremost ingredients in the Chinese repertoire.

4–5 lb (2 kg) duck	3 tablespoons Chinese rice wine or white wine
1 tablespoon soy sauce	
oil for frying	$\frac{1}{4}$ level teaspoon ground ginger
10 oz (275 g) can water chestnuts, drained	duck or chicken stock
	Sauce
1 bunch spring onions, trimmed and washed	2 tablespoons oyster sauce
	2 tablespoons sesame oil
1 inch (2$\frac{1}{2}$ cm) root ginger, peeled	2 tablespoons soy sauce
	1 level tablespoon cornflour
1 clove garlic	*Serves 4*

1 Rub the skin of the duck with soy sauce and leave to marinate for an hour or longer.

2 Heat enough oil in a wok or deep fryer to cover the duck. Turn the duck over a fairly high heat until brown on all sides, drain. (Alternatively brown in shallow depth of oil in a large frying pan.) Pour off the oil.

3 Add 2 tablespoons fresh oil to the wok or to a flameproof casserole, cook the water chestnuts for 15 seconds then strain.

4 Add the spring onions, ginger and garlic clove to the wok, then the wine, ground ginger and some stock. Return the duck to the wok or casserole, top up with stock, if necessary, and cook for 45 minutes.

5 If using a wok, now transfer the duck to a casserole, cutting it, if necessary, into portions, with *all* the vegetables. Add more stock if needed to cover the duck. Cover and simmer for a further 45 minutes, turning occasionally.

6 Remove the duck and set aside. Drain the vegetables and arrange on a serving dish, discarding the ginger and garlic. Cut the duck into serving pieces and arrange on the vegetables. Keep hot.

7 Combine the sauce ingredients with $\frac{1}{4}$ pint (150 ml) duck stock (fat removed). Bring to the boil, stirring, and allow to simmer for a minute. Pour over the duck and serve. Add a little extra stock if sauce is too thick.

Note To make this recipe easier, buy duck portions. Frying a whole duck is difficult if the frying receptacle is not large enough.

Fried Sea Bass

In China, eggs are considered as symbols of good luck and happiness. When a child is born, they are given as gifts, and always coloured red, symbol of luck and happiness. Eggs are used in cooking to bind food together and to add texture. Being an island, Hong Kong has a huge fishing fleet, and this next dish combines both eggs and sea bass.

About 2¼ lb (1 kg) generous weight of sea bass, filleted and skinned to give 1 lb (450 g) fillets	**Sauce**
	¼ pt (150 ml) Chinese rice wine or white wine
2 small eggs, beaten	1 tablespoon rice or wine vinegar
pinch of salt	1 tablespoon sesame oil
1 teaspoon sesame oil	1 level teaspoon cornflour
1 level teaspoon monosodium glutamate (optional)	2–3 spring onions, sliced
plain flour for dredging	
oil for deep frying	*Serves 4*

1 Slice the fish fillets diagonally across to make thin bite-size pieces. Dredge the fillets with flour.

2 Mix eggs, salt, sesame oil, monosodium glutamate (if used) in a small bowl. Add the fish and mix.

3 Heat the oil in a wok or deep fryer to 340°F (175°C). Try and maintain this temperature to ensure even frying.

4 Fry the fish a few pieces at a time depending on the size of wok. Cook until the fish pieces rise to the surface, turn them, if necessary, and cook until the batter is a light golden brown. Lift out with a draining spoon and place on kitchen paper. Keep hot while cooking remaining ingredients.

5 Carefully pour the oil out of the wok and add the wine, vinegar, sesame oil and cornflour. Bring to the boil, stirring, add the spring onions and 2 tablespoons of the oil used for frying the fish.

6 Stir well, pour into small bowls and serve with the fish.

●

West Lake Beef Soup

This is a meaty soup, well flavoured with fresh coriander, which is often used in Chinese cooking. If preferred, the quantity of beef may be reduced.

Marinade	$1\frac{3}{4}$ pints (950 ml) beef stock, or
1 level teaspoon cornflour	water and stock cubes
1 level teaspoon sugar	1 level teaspoon cornflour
1 teaspoon oil	3 tablespoons water
pinch of bicarbonate of soda	2 egg whites, lightly beaten
salt and pepper	$\frac{1}{2}$ oz (15 g) parsley or coriander,
Soup	chopped
1 lb (450 g) best minced beef	1 spring onion, sliced
4 tablespoons (3 fl oz) (75 ml) peanut or corn oil	
2 teaspoons Chinese rice wine or white wine	*Serves 4–6*

1 Mix the marinade ingredients in a bowl and stir in the beef. Leave overnight to tenderise the meat.

2 Turn the beef into a pan of boiling water, stir round to break up the pieces and cook for a few seconds to remove the marinade. Drain and reserve the meat.

3 Place 1 tablespoon oil in a wok with the wine and the stock, heat until boiling, add the beef and salt to taste. Blend the cornflour and water, stir into the soup to thicken. Cook for 15 minutes.

4 Remove pan from the heat, add the remaining oil, pour in the egg whites while stirring well, and sprinkle in parsley or coriander and spring onion. Continue cooking for a few seconds and serve.

●
Pineapple Fried Rice

In this dish, pork and fresh shrimps combine with the fruit, and the steamy rice absorbs the flavour of all three.

1 large pineapple, about 3 lb (2 kg)	2 spring onions, sliced
2 tablespoons oil	12 oz (350 g) pre-cooked long grain rice (see note)
4 oz (125 g) lean pork, finely chopped	4 oz (125 g) peeled prawns
2 eggs, beaten	salt

1 Place the pineapple on its side and cut off the other side to use as a lid. Scoop out the pineapple flesh, discarding the core. Chop about 8 oz (225 g) pineapple, and keep the rest for another use.

2 Heat the oil in a wok or frying pan and cook the pork for 10 seconds, stirring constantly. Drain the meat and put aside. Pour off most of the oil.

3 Stir in the eggs. Add the rice, prawns, spring onions and pineapple. Cook for 10 seconds tossing together, add the pork and continue to heat for $\frac{1}{2}$ minute, stirring and tossing the ingredients; add salt.

4 Spoon into the pineapple shell and cover with the lid so that the hot rice absorbs the flavour of the pineapple.

Note To make 12 oz (350 g) of cooked rice, cook 6 oz (175 g) rice in advance and leave to dry out for 24 hours before using for fried rice. Fresh cooked rice will be too lumpy.

_I_ndia

India is a sub-continent of many races, languages and religions. And that's the key to its food. North Indian food is as different from the cooking of Madras as Burgundian food is from that of Provence. In the North, the Moghul influence is strong – chapatis, parathas, puris, nan and other breads take the place of rice, which in the south of India is served throughout each meal.

In India, spices are blended specially for each dish using cardamom, cinnamon, saffron, nutmeg, turmeric, chillies, black peppercorns, cloves, ginger, and mustard seed. Curry powder is a dastardly British innovation which no self-respecting Indian cook would stoop to use – it's the equivalent of packet soup.

Traditionally Indian food is cooked with a kind of clarified butter known as _ghee_, but peanut oil, coconut oil, mustard oil and sesame oil are equally popular. When cooking Indian food it is best to set out all the ingredients in advance. In New Delhi, Simon Fernandes of the Ashoka Hotel created a menu for us based on his philosophy that 'excellence comes with experience and a continuing attention to detail – these, more than anything else, are the points I try to impart.'

Mutton Kofta Curry
Meatballs

In the whole of India you won't find a standard recipe for *koftas* or meatballs, which are usually made from goat meat, although ground lamb or beef make reasonable substitutes. 'Curry,' says Simon, 'isn't part of our vocabulary. The English word curry probably comes from the south Indian Tamil word for sauce, *kari*. It is also possible that the word derives from the *kari* leaf, a spice grown in India.'

Yogurt is used a great deal in Indian kitchens: 'It not only gives the sauce a creamy texture,' says Simon, 'but balances well with our pungent spices. Hardly a day goes by when we don't have yogurt in some form. For us it's a very important source of nutrition.'

Curry sauce	Koftas
1½ oz (40 g) butter or oil	1 egg
3 cloves garlic, crushed	1 lb (450 g) minced beef, mutton or
2 oz (50 g) onion, chopped finely	lamb
6 cardamom pods	½ level teaspoon salt
½ stick cinnamon	1 teaspoon fresh ginger, finely
2 tomatoes, chopped finely	grated
¼ teaspoon turmeric	1 clove garlic, crushed
¼ teaspoon chilli powder	⅛ teaspoon chilli powder
¼ teaspoon ground ginger	⅛ teaspoon ground coriander
¼ teaspoon ground coriander	2 oz (50 g) onions, finely chopped
pinch of salt	1 teaspoon fresh coriander, finely
½ pint (300 ml) natural yogurt	chopped
6 fl oz (175 ml) water	
freshly chopped coriander togarnish	*Serves 4–6* (Makes about 30 koftas)

1 Break the egg into a bowl and beat well, mix in the rest of the kofta ingredients, shape into about 30 even-sized meatballs.
2 Make the sauce: heat the butter or oil in a pan, add the garlic, onion, cardamom and cinnamon stick.

3 Add the tomatoes, spices and salt. Remove pan from the heat and gradually stir in the yogurt, so that each spoonful blends into the sauce before the next one and all the flavours are blended.

4 Add the meatballs to the sauce and simmer for about 30 minutes.

5 Lift the meatballs out of the sauce into a serving dish. Boil the sauce down a little and pour over the koftas, spear with cocktail sticks and serve as an appetiser.

6 Sprinkle with chopped coriander before serving.

Note These can also be used as a main course, and would be good served with plain boiled rice, the *sarsoon sag* and *aloo gobi* with *puri* as an accompaniment.

Puri
Fried bread puffs

One of the traditional breads of India is *puri*. The main ingredients are the same as *chapati* – flour and water – but with *puri*, the secret is to give the dough an elastic consistency so that it puffs up when fried. Other Indian breads are *paratha*, a shallow-fried, unleavened, wholewheat bread; *nan*, a flat, baked, leavened wholewheat bread; and *bhatura*, which is like a deep-fried *nan*.

4 oz (125 g) sieved wheatmeal flour	3½ fl oz (100 ml) water
4 oz (125 g) plain flour	oil for deep frying (1¼ pints approx)
pinch of salt	
2 tablespoons vegetable oil	*Makes 12*

1 Combine the flours and salt in a bowl, dribble in the oil and rub together with the fingertips to make the mixture resemble fine breadcrumbs.

2 Slowly add the water, so that the mixture forms a stiff pliable dough. Knead it until smooth using no extra flour.

3 Cover with a dribble of oil and put in a polythene bag or cling-film. Keep on one side for 30 minutes.

4 Knead again and divide mixture into 12 ball shapes, and keep these covered.

5 Flatten each piece and roll out to approximately 5 inches (13 cm) in diameter.

6 Heat the oil in a deep frying pan until hot, then carefully place a puri into the oil, being careful not to splash.

7 Push the puri carefully down into the hot oil with a slotted spoon, turn once and fry until golden brown.

8 Lift out and drain immediately on kitchen paper. Keep warm.

9 Continue working in this way until all are cooked, being careful of the oil.

10 Serve warm.

Aloo Gobi
Spiced potato and cauliflower

Pork is forbidden to Indian muslims; Hindus revere the cow as a symbol of the earth and a nourisher of life. The Hindu principle of *Ahimsa*, reverence for life, prohibits a large part of the population from killing animals for food. So, millions of Indians are vegetarians, and India has produced the most imaginative, varied and interesting vegetarian cuisine in the world. When cooked with imagination, even two such simple vegetables as potatoes and cauliflower can make a mouth-watering dish.

3 tablespoons oil	1 lb (450 g) potatoes, peeled and sliced like apples
$\frac{1}{4}$ teaspoon coriander seeds	
3 cardamom pods	salt and fresh black pepper
3 whole black peppercorns	2 tablespoons chopped fresh coriander
6 oz (175 g) tomatoes, chopped	
12 oz (375 g) white part cauliflower broken into florets	*Serves 6*

1 Heat the oil in a large frying pan, add the coriander seeds, cardamom pods and peppercorns. Lightly heat for a few seconds.

2 Stir in the tomato until blended, season with salt and freshly ground pepper.

3 Add the cauliflower and potatoes, stirring until mixed with the tomato mixture.

4 Cover and simmer for 15–20 minutes until the vegetables are just tender.

5 Sprinkle with chopped fresh coriander just before serving.

●

Sarsoon Sag
Mustard greens

In December the fields of sarsoon come into bloom. *Sarsoon* doesn't grow in England, but you can substitute fresh spinach or kale to make a reasonable facsimile. When making *sarsoon sag*, all of the seasonings should blend together so that one of them doesn't predominate over the others. 'The spices shouldn't taste raw either,' says Simon Fernandes. 'It is said that they shouldn't "catch in the throat". An unpardonable sin in cooking – a sin, I'm afraid, that is often committed in Western versions of our food. Taste, and never be afraid to adjust. Think of it as a form of fine tuning, perhaps like a violin.'

1 lb (450 g) sarsoon leaves, fresh spinach or kale	2 medium sized tomatoes, chopped
	salt
2 oz (50 g) unsalted butter	
1 dried chilli pepper	
½ teaspoon cumin seeds	**Garnish**
3 level tablespoons cornflour or finely ground cornmeal	slivers of fresh ginger and green chillies (optional)
1 teaspoon fresh ginger, finely grated	a little butter
	Serves 4–5

1 Prepare the vegetables by washing and removing stalks; chop.

2 Cook in boiling water until tender, drain well and purée. The result must be quite dry.

3 Melt the butter in a frying pan, crumble in the chilli and add the cumin seeds.

4 Stir in the cornflour, or cornmeal, then add the ginger and tomatoes and salt. Cook for 3–4 minutes.

5 Add the vegetable purée, stir round to absorb the sauce.

6 If liked, garnish with slivers of ginger and fresh chilli and a few knobs of butter.

● Mughlai Chicken

It was the Moghuls, descendants of the Ghengis Khan, sweeping into India over four hundred years ago, who first introduced meat to a basically vegetarian society. Moghul cuisine developed into the most elaborate form of cooking ever seen in India. From Moghul days come *tikka kebabs*, *shish kebabs*, and other kebabs which owe their origin to the Persian influence on north India.

One of the most famous dishes inherited from the Moghul era is *Mughlai* chicken. 'Chicken is a luxury. Lamb and goat meat are much more plentiful. So when we make chicken we treat it as a delicacy,' says Chef Fernandes.

2–3 lb (1 kg) chicken legs and breasts skinned and bones removed	**Sauce**
	1 stick cinnamon, crumbled
	6 cloves
2 eggs	4 oz (125 g) onions, finely chopped
2 cloves garlic, crushed	4 whole black peppercorns
1 tablespoon fresh ginger, finely grated	7 green cardamom pods
	3 cloves garlic, crushed
salt	3 tablespoons desiccated coconut
1 teaspoon garam masala (see note)	1½ teaspoons salt
	3 tablespoons poppy seeds, finely ground
4 fl oz (125 ml) vegetable oil	
	1 teaspoon fresh ginger, finely grated
Garnish	
	½ pint (300 ml) natural yogurt
sliced cashews and almonds (optional)	*Serves 4–6*

1 Flatten the chicken pieces a little.

2 Break the eggs onto a plate, mix in the garlic, ginger, salt and garam masala.

3 Dip the chicken pieces into the mixture to coat them thoroughly.

4 Heat the oil in a frying pan, add the chicken pieces and sauté until a golden brown. Remove and keep on one side.

To make the sauce

5 Add the whole spices to the oil in the pan to swell and very lightly colour them.

6 Stir in the onion and garlic and cook for a few minutes to blend the flavours, stir in the remaining ingredients except the yogurt.

7 Remove pan from the heat and gradually stir in half of the yogurt.

8 Return the chicken pieces to the sauce and simmer for a few minutes.

9 Arrange the chicken on a serving platter, add remainder of yogurt to the pan stirring well to blend in.

10 Spoon sauce over the chicken and, if liked, garnish with the cashews and almonds.

Note Garam masala is a blend of aromatic spices, such as black peppercorns, cumin seeds, cardamom pods, coriander seeds, whole cloves and cinnamon sticks. These spices can be ground in a blender and stored in an airtight container for 5–6 months. It is far better to make up your own mixture, but ready-made versions are available from Indian food shops.

Jalebis
Deep-fried pretzel-shaped sweets

Indians have a special fondness for sweets, and *jalebis* are among the most popular. *Jalebis* are said to be the test of a good cook. They should be light and crisp on the outside, yet warm and moist on the inside.

Dough	Syrup
6 oz (175 g) plain flour	½ pint (300 ml) water
⅛ teaspoon baking powder	12 oz (375 g) granulated sugar
7 fl oz (275 ml) warm water	2 tablespoons rose water
1 pint (600 ml) oil, approx.	

1 In a bowl combine the flour, baking powder and water, mix to a smooth batter.

2 Allow the mixture to rest for at least 4 hours.

3 Meanwhile, make the syrup; heat the water and sugar, stir until dissolved.

4 Cook quickly for about 5 minutes then add the rose water.

5 Pour into a wide shallow dish.

6 Heat the oil in a large deep frying pan.

7 Spoon the batter into the centre of a fairly large piece of calico. Bring the edges together so that it forms a 'money bag shape'. Cut a small hole in the bottom.

8 Quickly pipe pretzel or figure of eight shapes into the hot fat in lines from a slight height to help keep them thin.

9 Fry for 2 minutes, turning once until golden.

10 Remove with slotted spoon and put in the warm syrup.

11 Serve at once while warm and fresh.

Japan

The Japanese demand ingredients that are natural and as fresh as possible. They tend to cook their food lightly and often eat it raw. The appreciation of flavour and presentation is paramount. As one of Tokyo's leading chefs Nabuo Iida puts it: 'The glory of our cuisine lies in its simplicity. We cook without flourish, depending at all costs on freshness. Our few sauces are used to enhance, never disguise, flavours.'

Japanese meals are made up of many dishes served in modestly small portions. They begin with *zensai* or hors d'oeuvres, small chopstick-sized pieces of food meant to be eaten with *sake* or rice wine. Formal meals can have as many as twenty-six dishes. Because the Japanese are an ordered people, the succession of dishes follows a traditional pattern. As well as caring deeply about taste, the Japanese prize what they call *moritsuke* – the arrangement of food. Good chefs like Iida automatically think of colour, design and juxtaposition to bring out the beauty of food. 'For us, food must do more than simply ease hunger.' (See also introductory note to Hong Kong section.)

●

Wakadori Kuwayaki
Chicken in soy sauce

This dish is a particular favourite of Chef Iida. Serve with drinks or as part of a meal.

4 chicken leg quarters	1 tablespoon sake or medium dry sherry
1 level tablespoon plain flour	
1 tablespoon vegetable oil	1 tablespoon soy sauce
1 tablespoon mirin or sweet wine or sherry	$\frac{1}{2}$–2 teaspoons made-up Karashi or English mustard
	Serves 4–6

1 Remove chicken skins and cut meat off the bone. Cut into bite-sized pieces and toss in flour. Heat oil in a frying pan or wok, enough to coat the bottom of the pan. Add the chicken pieces and fry quickly, toss round with metal chopsticks or tongs until golden brown.

2 Lift out chicken pieces with a draining spoon into a sieve. Submerge briefly in lukewarm water to remove cooking oil.

3 Return the chicken to the pan. Add the mirin, sake, soy sauce and mustard. Stir round, add the chicken pieces and simmer until the sauce is syrupy and coats the chicken. Serve the chicken pieces on bamboo skewers or cocktail sticks.

Oshi Zushi
Pressed rice and mackerel

Japan is surrounded by some of the most fertile fishing grounds in the world, and over the years Japanese chefs have perfected the art of preparing fish in a dazzling variety of ways. 'Though we cook seafood in many ways – simmering, steaming, grilling, frying, just to name a few,' says Iida, 'I suppose raw fish, which we prepare in two basic forms, is of the greatest interest. First there is *sashimi*, a kind of hors d'oeuvre, and then *zushi*, which combines rice and raw fish. The key to both of these dishes is that the fish must be absolutely fresh. In fact, those who really appreciate *zushi* like to eat it at lunchtime, not only because it is light, but because lunch is closest to the time the fish arrive from the market.' *Oshi zushi* is a dish native to Osaka.

In Chinese supermarkets, it is possible to buy special white glutinous rice for this dish. Pudding rice would be better than long grain.

12 oz (350 g) short grain rice	2 small mackerel weighing about 2 lbs (900 g) filleted, skinned and cut into $\frac{1}{4}$ inch thick slices
about 1$\frac{1}{2}$ pints (800 ml) water	
$\frac{1}{2}$ level teaspoon salt	
1 level tablespoon sugar	**Garnish**
1 oz (25 g) cornflour	finely sliced and peeled root ginger
3 tablespoons rice or white wine vinegar	parsley
	Serves 6–8

1 Cook the rice in most of the water for 20–25 minutes. If rice dries before it is cooked, add the remaining water and extra water if necessary. Simmer until the rice is tender and the water has been absorbed. Drain well.

2 Mix the salt, sugar, cornflour and vinegar in a large bowl. Add the hot rice and toss to absorb the vinegar mixture. Toss and stir well to cool the rice quickly.

3 Line a large 3–4 pint loaf tin with cling-film and lightly press in the rice with the hand.

4 Remove any small bones from the mackerel, especially from the centre of the fillets. Neatly arrange the fish on the rice in one layer. Cover closely with cling-film and lightly press for at least 3 hours.

5 Remove weight and film, and turn out onto a plate or board. Remove film from sides and top, and cut into bite-sized pieces, wiping the knife with a wet cloth to make it easier. Garnish with thin slices of ginger and sprigs of parsley.

Note This can also be made with cooked prawns or smoked salmon.

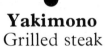

Yakimono
Grilled steak

The ingredients for the next dish are fillets of *Kobe* beef, mushrooms, asparagus and two oranges. Just as the Japanese learnt the art of tea making from the Chinese and the art of frying food from the Portuguese, so it wasn't until Japan was flooded with Western businessmen in the 1860s after two centuries of isolation that they developed an interest in meat. Today *Kobe* beef, richly marbled with fat, is amongst the most highly regarded in the world. Some suggest that *Kobe* beef is the tenderest, because the cattle are often massaged and given beer to drink; leading a very placid life they don't develop any hard muscles the way free-ranging prairie cattle do.

1½ lb (675 g) fillet of beef or sirloin steak in one piece	2½ fl oz (75 ml) mirin or sweet wine or sherry
10 small fresh flat mushrooms, stalks removed and lightly scored	2½ fl oz (75 ml) sake or medium dry sherry
8 oz (225 g) fresh asparagus	finely grated rind of 2 oranges (to give 1 tablespoon)
Sauce	
¼ pint (150 ml) soy sauce	*Serves 4–6*

1 Prepare the sauce: bring soy sauce, mirin and sake to boil in a small saucepan and simmer uncovered for 10 minutes. Pour into a shallow dish to cool. Sprinkle in the grated orange rind.

2 Trim the meat of any fat and cut into $\frac{1}{2}$ inch (1 cm) thick slices. Place in the sauce to marinate for 10–15 minutes, turning occasionally.

3 Score the mushrooms and thread onto long skewers. Thread asparagus onto skewers.

4 Prepare a hot grill. Place meat, mushrooms and asparagus on grill rack or pan, and brush vegetables with mirin. Cook for 1–2 minutes on each side or until cooked to taste. Brush all with marinade if they become dry.

●

Tempura
Batter-fried food

Tempura is *the* fried food of Japan. The batter is lighter than anything you'll find elsewhere. Shrimps, fish, prawns, aubergines, carrots, sweet potatoes, onion rings, green beans, mushrooms and green peppers are all batter fried and are delicious served golden hot.

2 egg yolks	Soy sauce or a dipping sauce
$\frac{1}{2}$ pint (300 ml) iced water	
8 oz (225 g) plain flour	
oil for deep frying	
A selection of bite-size pieces of raw fish and meat, slices of aubergine, carrot, potato, sprigs of broccoli, small mushrooms, etc.	(This batter is sufficient for enough ingredients to serve 3–4 as a main course)

1 Beat the egg yolks in a bowl with the iced water. (The coldest water possible is the secret of light batter.) Add the flour all at once and gradually beat in until it forms a smooth thick batter. Place a little extra flour on a plate.

2 Heat the oil in a wok or deep fryer to 340°F (175°C). Try and maintain this temperature to ensure even frying.

3 Dip each piece lightly in a little flour and then into the batter. Drain lightly and place in the hot oil. Cook for about 3 minutes until the batter is a light golden brown, turning to cook evenly. Lift out with a draining spoon and put on kitchen paper. Keep hot, while cooking the remaining ingredients. Cook the fish or meat ingredients a few pieces at a time, and then the vegetables.

4 While frying, pick out the pieces of batter that come loose in the oil. This keeps the oil from getting heavy.

5 Serve immediately with a sauce.

Note If only cooking a few ingredients, halve the batter quantities.

Dipping sauces are available in bottles from supermarkets e.g. oyster, mushroom ketchup, soy sauce, chilli and barbecue. Put on the table in small dishes. To test for the temperature, cook a cube of bread in the oil – it should sizzle and start browning lightly at once.

●

Kamo Nabe
Cook-it-yourself duck

Japanese cooking is famous for its *nabemuno* or one-pot dishes. Guests sit round a table and cook together in a communal pot. *Kamo nabe*, or wild duck pot, is a *nabemuno* dish made from a wild duck the Japanese call *hongamo* and a variety of vegetables.

Chef Iida pays particular attention to the cutting of vegetables. In Japan every action has an almost symbolic function. 'How we cut and slice vegetables has a definite purpose – to use the particular shape that responds best to the nature of the vegetable and at the same time enhances its flavour. None of our cutting is random.'

A Japanese kitchen is almost as clinical and as clean as an operating theatre; there is an emphasis on order and visual appeal. The ingredients must look as attractive when they are being prepared as they will be when served at table.

4–5 lb (2 kg) duck	A few sprigs of fresh coriander or parsley
1 egg yolk	
1 tablespoon soy sauce	**Sauce for cooking**
A selection of raw vegetables such as bite-size pieces of carrot, celery, canned bamboo shoots, spring onions, radishes and button mushrooms, all very thinly sliced	12 fl oz (375 ml) chicken stock
	4 fl oz (100 ml) mirin or sweet wine
	4 tablespoons sake or dry sherry
	4 tablespoons soy sauce
	Serves 4

1 Carefully remove all the flesh from the duck, discarding the skin and carcass. Slice the breast fillets into bite-size thin slices and keep on one side. Finely mince the remaining meat and mix with the egg yolk and soy sauce. Form into loose dumplings about the size of a small walnut.

2 Heat all the sauce ingredients to simmering point in a large pot or cast iron casserole or small saucepan. Adjust the heat, so that the sauce simmers throughout the cooking.

3 Add the items carefully to the stock, a few pieces at a time, starting with the dumplings, then the vegetables, then the breast pieces. Simmer in the sauce until cooked to taste, about 4–5 minutes for the duck.